Jubilee Economics

JUBILEE ECONOMICS

The Purpose, Practices, and Possibilities for a Better Future

Kelley Nikondeha

Maryknoll, New York 10545

Founded in 1970, Orbis Books endeavors to publish works that enlighten the mind, nourish the spirit, and challenge the conscience. The publishing arm of the Maryknoll Fathers and Brothers, Orbis seeks to explore the global dimensions of the Christian faith and mission, to invite dialogue with diverse cultures and religious traditions, and to serve the cause of reconciliation and peace. The books published reflect the views of their authors and do not represent the official position of the Maryknoll Society. To learn more about Maryknoll and Orbis Books, please visit our website at www.orbisbooks.com.

Copyright © 2026 by Kelley Nikondeha.

Published by Orbis Books, Box 302, Maryknoll, NY 10545-0302.

Unless otherwise noted, scripture quotations are taken from the New Revised Standard Version Updated Edition. Copyright © 2021 National Council of Churches of Christ in the United States of America. Used by permission. All rights reserved worldwide.

All rights reserved.

No part of this publication may be reproduced or transmitted in any form or by any means, electronic or mechanical, including photocopying, recording, or any information storage or retrieval system, without prior permission in writing from the publisher.

Queries regarding rights and permissions should be addressed to: Orbis Books, P.O. Box 302, Maryknoll, NY 10545-0302.

Manufactured in the United States of America.

Manuscript editing and typesetting by Joan Weber Laflamme.

Library of Congress Cataloging-in-Publication Data

Names: Nikondeha, Kelley, 1969– author
Title: Jubilee economics : the purpose, practices, and possibilities for a better future / Kelley Nikondeha.
Identifiers: LCCN 2025024187 (print) | LCCN 2025024188 (ebook) | ISBN 9781626986350 trade paperback | ISBN 9798888660904 epub
Subjects: LCSH: Distributive justice—Religious aspects—Christianity | Distributive justice—Religious aspects—Judaism | Economics—Religious aspects—Christianity | Economics—Religious aspects—Judaism | Jubilee (Judaism)
Classification: LCC BR115.J8 N545 2026 (print) | LCC BR115.J8 (ebook)
LC record available at https://lccn.loc.gov/2025024187
LC ebook record available at https://lccn.loc.gov/2025024188

*For practitioners at home and abroad,
may this book be good company,
offering generative conversation amid
the ebbs and flows of your emancipatory efforts.*

*For those formed by the jubilary work of Walter Brueggemann,
may we honor his memory by living as a
"testimony to the otherwise"
in a world of exploitive economies and incessant injustice.*

Contents

Introduction 1

Part One
The Purpose of Jubilee

1. Prehistory of Jubilee 15
2. Jubilee Canon 29
3. Jubilee Campaign 45

Part Two
The Practices of Jubilee

4. Loan Practices 63
5. Labor Practices 79
6. Land Practices 93

Part Three
The Possibilities of Jubilee

7. Loss and Lament 111
8. Hope and Hard Work 125
9. The New City and the Work of Imagination 143

Acknowledgments 165

Introduction

On a crisp Sunday morning in Bujumbura, the capital of the small East African country of Burundi, my husband called me. I answered the call from our home in the United States, where I spent the school year with our children. I reveled in the sounds of Burundian birdsong I could hear in the background as he sat at the kitchen table of our small apartment in the heart of Africa. He regaled me with tales from the previous day. Our conversation took on a mix of family news, updates from the field, and decisions to be made about the fledgling bank founded just six months earlier. Our unconventional partnership regularly had us on different continents for months at a time, yet we remained in the thick of shared conversations and tandem work in the community development space.

As we spoke, Claude's second phone began ringing. Ignoring it, we carried on our conversation about securing a tract of land in Bubanza province for the Batwa community. Then it rang again. Once more he tried to disregard it, staying focused on the matter at hand. When his phone rang again, and his third phone buzzed, I said: "Something's going on, Claude. Find out what it is and call me back later." A man who needs three phones obviously receives many calls, so this interruption was not new. Even so, the frenzy of calls on a Sunday morning when most people were getting ready for church, not work, was odd.

Within minutes Claude called back. There was a fire burning at the central market, not far from the apartment. "I can see the smoke from here," he reported, stepping out on the patio. "I'm going to walk there and see what's happening."

As usual, his desire was to get straight to the center of what was happening. In his earlier professional life he was the Anderson Cooper of Burundi, reporting on the civil war from the field and then anchoring the nightly news broadcast on Burundi's single television channel. So he set off on foot to once again search out the story—as well as check on our bank members who sold their wares there.

Within the ten-acre labyrinth of tiny stalls all tightly jammed together you could find everything: purses, shoes, tools, cooking oil, school supplies, housewares, and car parts imported from India and China and beyond. The first time I entered the maze was with my mother-in-law, Mama Rose. Hunting for ingredients for upcoming meals, she bobbed and weaved through the narrow spaces, pushing around others with a kind of practiced grace I had trouble mimicking as I tried to keep up. She took us past all the stalls under the corrugated metal roof, out to an open area filled with fruits, vegetables, and local herbs.

She introduced me to her favorite vendors for tomatoes, onions, and mandarins, and found the woman with the best mangos to indulge my cravings. We wove our way out through another outdoor space filled with squawking chickens, cages holding rabbits, butcher stalls with meat hanging on hooks, and tables piled high with various fish from Lake Tanganyika.

The smells, sounds, and sheer variety of things all under one steel roof at the central marketplace overwhelmed my Western senses.

My fondest memories of the marketplace center around my incessant quest for the signature African block fabrics, awash with bright colors and bold patterns, on daily display as women wore them in both traditional and modern designs. Claude's aunt, Leonie, took me many times to the corner of the market dedicated to textiles where ladder-like racks leaned against the walls and allowed vibrant bolts of fabric to climb the wall in a mosaic as high as the eyes could see. Women used long broomstick-like rods to pull chosen bolts down for our closer inspection. Later, when I went with my sisters-in-law, they made it a social outing. We'd visit their friends working various stalls, exchanging stories along with a little economic transaction. I began to discern the song pulsating through this place, the laughter weaving through the cacophony of lives and livelihoods.

Outside the marketplace rows of buses, mini and full sized, cycled through the large lot because the central market complex functioned as the makeshift bus station. Since this is where most people needed to go to work or to shop, all roads led to and from it. Even if you didn't go in, you found yourself on the periphery grabbing a soda or buying phone credit from a vendor as you waited to catch your bus home. It truly was central to the life of the city.

It was also, without doubt, the economic engine of the capital city. This market served as the epicenter of all the other rural markets, where women and men would come to buy imported goods and in turn sell in their community markets up-country. It kept products moving in from the port and out through the rural network, and Burundian francs followed suit. Of course the central market also had money changers, beggars, thieves, and even a small crew of firefighters with a single yellow fire engine—though no one knows where it was on the Sunday morning it was most needed.

As Claude followed the dark smoke, he was not alone. Some rushed to the scene hoping it was a small fire and they could quickly salvage their inventory and money boxes. Others ran looking for family members working the skeleton shift before church or possibly trapped in the lockup. Most came out of curiosity. What was breaking the peace of a quiet Sunday morning, the only time the central market ever slept? As the flames reached higher and higher, the crowds watched as flames engulfed the market. Vendors watched as their kiosks became kindling. The metal roof heaved, as if grasping for air, then slowly sagged under the extreme heat. Within hours it took its final pose, crumpled like sheet of paper in the middle of a shocked city.

During those hours Claude called me several times. We knew the gravity of the situation. What this would do to the city, to the economy, to families watching the flames consume their businesses. I thought of the women making a living there day in and day out, the butchers and fish mongers, our family friends, those who banked with us, and the big personalities all bent with fear as the fire raged. It felt so personal.

"They're losing everything," Claude said. "It's just all burning." He knew these women and men by name. They came to Kazoza Bank hoping to find help not usually on offer to the unbanked. They shared their dreams with him—and he took a chance on them. And honestly, they took a chance on us and our newly approved bank. As the central market burned, we were all at a loss, together.

"Will we survive?" I finally asked. Compared to what our clients faced, it felt like the wrong question at the wrong time. And yet, starting this bank and funding these women and men had been the lion's share of our work for the past eighteen months. Were all our efforts and hopes going up in smoke, too? Could we recover from this?

"Over 70 percent of our clients have kiosks in the central market," Claude said. That meant 70 percent of the loans the bank had given would most likely not be paid back—how could they be, after such a catastrophic loss?

"So this is the end of Kazoza Bank?" I asked in disbelief.

The answering silence on the other end of the line shook me.

For years we had talked about financial principles and considered our faith and values as central to our work, looking to contemporary ideas based in justice as well as ancient biblical economic methods, among them, the practice of jubilee. "Isn't jubilee," I said, "something for this very moment?" I continued, seeking a solution in real time. "If the biblical economic program means anything, it must be something that offers direction now as we stand on the cusp of economic ruin. Right?"

Again, I was met by silence.

"Shouldn't we be talking about canceling all those loans as jubilee instructs?" I pressed, recalling some of the specific details of the jubilee plans instituted by judges, kings, and ancient leaders. "The jubilee texts clearly direct economic policies for times like this."

Finally Claude spoke. "But as a financial institution credentialed by the Central Bank," he noted, "we are not allowed to zero out those loans. We would lose our certificate to operate *at all* if we canceled the debt."

"So that means jubilee can't apply—doesn't apply—here?" I became the silent one. Were we in territory beyond the scope of jubilee? As the theologian of this duo, an impasse like this was a jarring prospect.

For a community leader and practitioner like Claude the fire was making ashes of his aspirations, a vivid reminder that despite all our best efforts for the bank, we could not guarantee that things will work. Sometimes the truth on the ground is unforgiving, dashing our highest hopes of helping others.

His loud exhale told me we might be at the end of the road as far as the bank was concerned.

In Kirundi, Burundi's national language, the word *kazoza* means "good future." Today that felt like a cruel joke. We thought we could be part of a good future for families usually left out of the economy—perhaps the joke was on us. Instead of our boats rising together, they were sinking side by side.

Thousands of miles away I felt as deflated as that massive metal roof, as my own sadness gave way to tears. How could the fire be allowed to burn and rob families of their livelihood? How could Kazoza Bank be done? How could jubilee not be a reality for this moment? That night I tossed and turned, unable to sleep, unable accept the limitations of our work—and of jubilee, something I'd believed was created for times like these.

The next morning Claude went to his office at Kazoza Bank. Around forty women crowded around the gates of the bank. As he walked toward them, he could hear the crying. He told the guard to open the gate, then directed the women to the back patio. Under usual circumstances the large covered space hosted training sessions and staff meetings. But not today.

The women sat. One stood up, looked at Claude, and said, "Yesterday morning I woke up as a business woman. Last night, I went to bed poor." Another started to share about what she lost in the fire—her kiosk, all her inventory, and her tiny cash box with money she'd yet to deposit. There was a chorus of "me, too" from around the circle. Some women doubled over with groans. Cries continued. Tears flowed. The sorrow moved throughout the patio as if in surround sound.

Some of the staff peeked out the office windows. One came out and whispered in Claude's ear, asking if he should escort the women out. After all, it's not good for business to have loud and animated wailing as other clients come through the front door. But Claude countered, "Go get donuts and some cases of soda. And tell all the other staff to bring more chairs and join us here. There is no other business today but this."

And so for the next set of hours, the women shared their losses one by one. They detailed what the flames took from them. They cried at all their work—the training, the loan interviews, the applications for kiosks, the daily shifts at the market—amounting to nothing in the shadow of Sunday. Many wondered how they could recover, not sure they could start again. The staff listened. They went out and got more donuts and soda. The women mourned and tried to comfort one another. Claude cried. That day no one was rushed out or forced to answer any questions about what would be next. They were given space to weep, and the Kazoza team wept with them.

Meanwhile, across the ocean, I wondered how a practice Claude and I were so heavily invested in could fall short in this moment. I looked deeper for something we might have missed. I printed out all the jubilee texts from Leviticus, Deuteronomy, Isaiah, and Luke. I pulled commentaries off my shelves to refreshed my memory and check my own work on the ancient context and meaning of the jubilee concept. I began to pour over the scriptures in a kind of manic meditation. If we cannot legally cancel the debt, is our jubilee practice null and void? Is there a way to enact jubilee without violating Burundian law? Or maybe, I thought, our understanding of these texts is too constricted. What if we looked for larger economic movement in the jubilary construct?

This is when Claude and I, the practitioner and the theologian, began to cut our teeth on the jubilee texts found in scripture. Our attempt to take these texts seriously while running a local community bank serving the working poor put jubilee to the ultimate test in the months following the marketplace fire.

For us, these conversations were not abstract, but practical and personal.

Of course, our jubilee conversations affected more than Kazoza Bank. They informed nearly all our development enterprises—how we designed our porridge factory to address malnourishment, why we worked to release "patient prisoners" at a local hospital, how we addressed the deforestation of the national park, and how we understood the need for economic development for communities living in and around the depleted land.

We quickly began to understand that while debt cancellation is central to jubilary practice, it is *more* than merely debt cancellation. Jubilee is also about land, labor, and other landscapes of liberation. In their ancient and biblical heyday the policies embodied justice. And we determined to embrace that kind of tangible justice in our work in Burundi. So, naturally, our jubilary practice intersected with our various development enterprises the way the economy in any place and time intersects with almost all areas of our lives.

Looking back, I admit my initial investigation of the jubilee texts in scripture were wooden, two-dimensional, reading the Hebrew Bible texts of Leviticus and Deuteronomy saying to cancel all debts, then trying to force a literal reading onto our current economy. Until the marketplace fire, I indulged that way of interpretation looking for straightforward application. Now, confronted with the reality modern banking and local economics, I faced the choice before me. I could accept that jubilee was consigned to an ancient past, as many did. Or I could wrestle with scripture until it yielded an insight and a meeting of practice with ethics. I opted for the later, and together with the practitioner in Claude, we discovered a more expansive understanding of the jubilee program and a more vibrant economic, banking, community practice as a result.

This did not happen quickly; nor did it happen alone. Over the next ten years we expanded our jubilee practices with a fair amount of trial and error. Claude tested, tried, and tweaked. He applied his entrepreneurial instincts with creativity on the ground. I read more widely and deeper. I meditated on the scriptures at hand from a variety of angles and asked fresh questions that sprouted from our work. Through a long season of cross-pollination between the Burundian context and the jubilee canon of scripture new vistas in jubilary understanding emerged.

Now our jubilee conversations are fundamental to our community development work and how we endeavor to enact tangible transformation. They also have shaped our family conversations around how we want to show up in our world. Whether speaking with the president of Burundi or our nextdoor neighbors, we engage as jubilee practitioners. And while economies are fickle and fragile things, these jubilee conversations offer some ancient, sturdy hooks to begin real discussions about economic practices that move toward equity and the common good. These are worthwhile conversations for national and international entities, businesses, churches, families, and neighbors—because we all live in and must navigate our economies. We are not merely victims of economic landscapes, but practitioners with agency on these economic footpaths we daily tread. For instance, how we manage debt matters to us and our neighbors. Are we burdened with an unsustainable debt load pressuring us to compromise our compassion or neighborliness, to make choices against our values? Do we weaponize debt in our business or politics? Can we structure loans that bring freedom to those in our community? Do our economic practices entangle or emancipate others from cycles of indebtedness and loss? If we find ways to engage that are ethical, just, and responsible, we will offer our communities tangible hope for the future and real relief in the present.

This book explores the purpose, practices, and possibilities of jubilee economics in a time of fragile economies and looming economic shifts. What Claude and I have learned on the field and through study of jubilee provides language for better conversations about what it means to shape a more just economy. It showcases an array of tools on offer for those working to cultivate more equitable communities, economic and otherwise. It cracks open our imaginations to consider fresh possibilities in the face of calcified modalities.

Jubilee conversations also offer us the opportunity to speak honestly about the economies in which we live. We can talk about the precarity of our local economy honestly, as jubilee texts do. We can bring into focus tools to try or tweak in addressing challenges our communities face. Jubilee suggests we consider debt, land ownership and inheritance, labor and fair wages as conversation starters. We might add that entrepreneurship and creative responses to economic conditions are also within the jubilee purview, following the example of those biblical authors and key figures who innovated ancient debt cancellation policies to forge jubilee canon. This collection of economic wisdom is far from arcane; instead, it brims with relevance for our current conversations about cultivating greater equity in our societies. And just as jubilee has come to connote celebration in our modern vernacular, we absolutely have reason to celebrate this body of economic literature and embrace it in our own community-building, community-sustaining endeavors.

Rather than allowing fear to dominate conversations around money, debt, employment, and inheritance, we can counter with more hopeful content—not utopian notions that make us feel good, but that we secretly suspect will never move the economic needle in reality (and maybe never did). We can reach for tangible, practical tools that have been tried for centuries and found to be true for the courageous practitioner. Instead of feeding fear, we can opt for curiosity about the earliest practices around debt relief, economic renewal, and property management to glean fresh perspective and practical tools to test. There are good conversations on offer for those working to forge more just communities. Jubilee gives us ancient threads to pull, tenured conversations to continue for generative purpose.

With julibary verve, we can question the status quo. Yes, another way to engage in the economy *is* possible—one that eschews exploitation, perpetual indebtedness, joblessness, forfeiture as the norm, permanent poverty cycles, and other variations on economic injustice that riddle our communities. Jubilee invites our imaginations to break free and enter into generative thinking as we confront economic challenges faced by our families, communities, and even countries. We can work hard at new modes of engagement and do so with tangible hope that something different is possible. And as we become jubilee practitioners in our communities, we become what theologian Walter Brueggemann calls "a testimony to the otherwise." Just economies that foster viable and vibrant prospects for our families and neighbors and fellow citizens are worth contending for with all our jubilary energy.

∼

As Claude wept with the women who'd lost everything in the marketplace fire, something stirred deep within his practitioner's soul. *These women cannot be left like this, bent with such loss. They cannot be reduced to poverty again. There must be another future on offer for them. And we need to be part of that work—whether or not we call it jubilee.* He was no longer married to the concept; he was committed to an outcome. *If jubilee can be of service, it will have to do heavy lifting to raise these women from the ashes.*

And so Claude threw down the gauntlet. We immediately got busy imagining ways to get these women back into the economy. This was no solitary project. It was a community's challenge across many months that including our Kazoza Bank staff and all our friends working together in their various capacities on a series of initiatives to embody the highest aspirations of jubilee.

We put jubilee to the test. And we continue to put jubilee to the test in other contexts. For the sake of real women, real people trapped in extreme poverty, we put these biblical concepts to work in a modern economy finding that transformation is possible. It is slow, but possible.

These jubilee conversations continue to fund our thinking, our imaginations, and our daily practice in our development enterprises. I invite you to join the jubilee conversation—and see how this can come to life in your own life and community.

Part One

The Purpose of Jubilee

1

Prehistory of Jubilee

I asked, "Claude, do you remember all those workshops we taught on jubilee over the years and people would ask if there was actually proof jubilee was ever practiced? I imagine our call for economic engagement rooted in debt forgiveness could be more easily dismissed for want of biblical, historical, receipts."

What Claude recalled was that it was often a *muzungu*, a Westerner, asking that question. "Africans never asked that question. If it's in scripture, or if it's ancient wisdom tradition, we accept it. Debt forgiveness and other economic practices in the Good Book might come as a surprise. But once we see it, we want to do it. We want to get busy making it happen in our communities."

We reminisced about seminars in Uganda, Kenya, and South Africa where the jubilee conversations popped and crackled with ideas around local implementation of what we understood to be a biblical imperative toward economic equity. Those community leaders weren't looking for an excuse to ignore jubilee. "You're right," I said to Claude. "They wanted new tools to try in their communities—and what could be better than economic tools engineered within the biblical story?"

"The question was irrelevant to me, honestly," he said."If Jesus spoke of jubilee as good news for his community, then I believed it could be possible for mine in Burundi. My question was *how*. How do I make jubilee freedom a reality for our Batwa friends on the margins of society? How do I bring jubilee relief to the unbanked in Bujumbura who are locked out of the economy? And it got very real when I sat with the women that Monday morning after the marketplace fire. That day the question shifted from *how* to *if*. Not if it happened in scripture, but if jubilee could still happen in Burundi in the aftermath of the fire."

Before the fire our primary question was how to implement jubilee. The intent of jubilee was enough to fund our imagination and fuel our work. *If* never was part of our initial landscape of questions. Perhaps we were naive. But after the fire we wrestled with whether jubilee could still be a load-bearing economic practice in the face of our massive loss. That question pushed us to dig deep. We were not looking to opt out, but to hold jubilee to account.

But I remember the last time I was in Burundi hosting Western friends. The small group gathered in Claude's office. His standing desk became a makeshift pulpit as I taught them about jubilee economics as the foundation for our community development enterprise. One man, a successful businessman, kept shifting side to side as I spoke. His discomfort was visible.

Finally he asked the inevitable question: "They never really canceled debts, though, right?" He intuitively knew what it might mean for him and his business dealings if jubilee was a biblical principle he was expected to practice. The cost of jubilee was thinking differently about debt, land foreclosure, and workers' wages—and he knew it.

So, as I've answered many other *muzungus* before him, I said that there is ample evidence of debt cancellation when we look at jubilee practitioners woven throughout the fabric of scripture, Jesus included. I see enough in the text to give me confidence that jubilee was both taught and practiced. Then, as now, I offer no relief from the discomfort—because that is a legitimate part of jubilee.

Prehistory of Jubilee

But as a theologian, this question circles back often. I confront it in books and commentaries, in lectures and sermons, even in the seminars we convene. People want receipts. They want to know that this was practiced in the promised land, in David's kingdom, in Galilee when Jesus walked those dusty streets. Unless there is proof, there is a plausible deniability perhaps.

Those longed-for receipts? The good news is that we do have them. And more are being found. Recent publications from historians, economists, and archeologists have arrived at a shared conclusion—debt cancellation was an ancient economic practice. That means we need to talk about jubilee differently and practically. And we need to stretch the conversation back to debt cancellation in earlier civilizations as we begin our exploration of this biblical practice.

~

It matters where you start the conversation. If you begin the jubilee conversation with the biblical canon, you miss the root system of the very human struggle with debt and how that is a formative part of discussions about human survival. The first vocation of humanity is to survive, and often we overlook how critical that is in the development of our species. Our ancestors worked hard to subsist in less than ideal conditions, conditions that included local economics managing wages, taxes, and debt. Debt is part of our human condition. So are precarious economies in need of constant calibration.

Debt is not only a modern matter. The burden of individual indebtedness and the ways collective debt calcified an imperial economy were part of ancient realities too. Debt is as old as civilization itself, as our oldest archeological artifacts put on display. Early survival strategies our ancestors tried their hands at to curb debt and promote thriving economies got handed down to us, their descendants. We walk in these footsteps as we consider jubilee.

Our ancestors birthed good things in Sumer, Babylon, and Assyria. Their struggle gave rise to generative practices and conversations about economic realities. For so long these dynamics were lost to us, as the proverbial sands of time covered their tracks. We thought early economic epochs were littered with local barter, long trade routes, and other primitive modalities. But now historians and archeologists have unearthed critical accounts demonstrating that economic conversations were complex and challenging from the beginning.[1] And these discoveries offer us the opportunity to honor our ancestors as savvy economic practitioners worthy of our respect and their ideas as worth revisiting.

∽

The ruler of Lagash, Enmetena, stands as the first recorded person to practice debt cancellation to bring relief to his kingdom. Lagash was a prominent city-state in Sumer in the third millennium BCE, and one of its earliest kings of record was Enmetena. We learn of him leading the army of Lagash in response to a border dispute with neighboring city-state Umma. Initially Lagash was victorious over Umma and ended the conflict by exacting tribute. But soon after, Umma cut the water supply to Lagash, provoking another season on the battlefield. After a series of such skirmishes, Lagash was ultimately triumphant. The success came with a treaty brokered by Enmetena to preserve the welfare of both entities. The resulting thirty years of peace became one of the most lasting legacies of Enmetena.

As part of the peace negotiations, Enmetena forgave the tribute Umma owed Lagash. And when he returned home and surveyed the condition of his people, he had a similar inclination. He understood that war impoverished soldiers and

---

[1] For a comprehensive exploration of the history of debt that sheds light on the true nature of our earliest economies and the development of credit, debt, and such, see David Graeber, *Debt: The First 5000 Years* (Melville House, 2014).

their families, and the years of warfare had exacted a toll. So he announced the cancellation of debts pertaining mainly to crop rents and fees owed to the palace. But the announcement also meant that people were freed to return to their homes, to their families, after having been sold as debt slaves during the war years.

This is called an *amargi proclamation*. The term comes from two words meaning "mother" and "to return" respectively. When combined, *amargi* gives the meaning of a return to the mother condition or original state of things.[2] Imagine the original state as the time before falling into catastrophic indebtedness. Such an edict was the good news of freedom from literal debt bondage to creditors. But some translators note the quite literal meaning—a return to a mother—leads us to consider children sold into debt slavery released back into the arms of their family. This is the first record of many *amargi* edicts we have discovered, thanks to the tireless work of some archeologists.

While this *amargi* proclamation is the first debt cancellation we have on record, dated at 2400 BCE, this was likely not the first *amargi* proclamation in Sumer. On display from the proclamation are our earliest human records, including testimonies to the practice of debt cancellation as a tool for addressing times of economic peril. *Amargi* records also functioned as tools in brokering peace treaties and repairing the land of both aggressor and victim in the aftermath of wars. Imagine that—not leaving the enemy destitute! Leaving the conquered destitute only became an accepted practice of war in the Classic Era, perfected by Rome.[3]

This ancient incident from Lagesh, complete with an archeological artifact, describes a time when debts were annulled not only to balance an economy or prop up a regime but to offer

---

[2] Michael Hudson, . . . *And Forgive Us Our Debts: Lending, Foreclosure, and Redemption from Bronze Age Finance to the Jubilee Year* (Islet-Verlag, 2018), 76–77.

[3] Hudson, 78.

restoration to all. It demonstrates debt amnesty connected to a deep humanity.

∼

Our own excavation work also begins with Enmetena and his economic relief work in Lagash. This is where we begin to see the origin story of jubilee unfold. We can now witness a flurry of financial developments, regular bouts of indebtedness, and periodic debt cancellation thanks to recent scholarship in fields of Assyriology, archeology, and history.[4]

Traveling further back to our first recorded human interactions we find, not only myths and religious writings, but records of interest-bearing debt and accounting. The earliest recovered Mesopotamian documents reveal economic activity and proof of an era of economic development, with advances in interest-bearing debts, accounting, currency creation, and other commercial enterprises. These were initiated and innovated in the institutions of the palace and temple of early civilizations.[5]

As happens now, external factors often impinged on ancient economies. A famine, or drought, or some other natural disaster, or perhaps a manmade one like war, would knock the economy off balance. As these large-scale changes changed economies and people's fragile place within them, this landed a majority of people in a state of indebtedness, unable to pay or repay the temple and the palace taxes, rents, and fees. But rather than allow the populous to fall prey to creditors, to risk losing their land or freedom, the palace would enact widespread debt cancellation. This practice also allowed people to stay and contribute to local economies rather than be tempted to migrate elsewhere for a new start. Keeping the labor force in place and available for building projects and miliary service contributed to a return to a revitalized, stable economy. In

---

[4] For those interested in exploring the history in greater depth, I highly recommend Hudson.

[5] Hudson, xx.

Prehistory of Jubilee

short, these debt cancellation initiatives kept economic equilibrium in our earliest civilizations.

Assyriologists were the first to trace jubilee practice to the tradition of royal debt cancellations, the *amargi*, from Sumer in the third millennium BCE.[6] As a new ruler would ascend to the throne, he would proclaim justice, which meant all personal debts owed to the government (palace and temple) were annulled.[7] No doubt the immediate write-off of all debt added to the air of celebration for all. But it also meant the reign of the sovereign began with balanced books.

A new change in reign, however, was not the only time for the ancient civilizations' historical widespread debt forgiveness. When the economy experienced constriction or calcification due to a natural disaster that affected harvest yields, or perhaps following a war, a ruler could—and often would—proclaim justice. All personal debts would be annulled. The records of such proclamations are part of our earliest history, reaching back to Sumer.

∼

The Bronze Age continues with the story of Babylon, and Hammurabi, who ruled from 1792 BCE to 1750 BCE. This name is familiar to us due to the Code of Hammurabi, the well-known collection of 282 laws that first and famously established the presumption of innocence in law for the accused as well as limits on retribution demanded by victims. So legendary are these laws that we find Hammurabi's likeness commemorated

---

[6] Hudson, xiv.

[7] It is interesting that the declaration to *practice justice* was, in the earliest human records, a call to cancel debts. It was a real practice about real debts; that is what *justice* looked like from the beginning. This is true of the Hebrew Bible as well. The mention of doing justice is most often about economic actions, not judicial ones. Justice in the Hebrew Bible is better understood as economics, not as a tool or product of law enforcement. More about this can be found in the works of Walter Brueggemann.

in the chamber of the US House of Representatives and on the southern wall of the US Supreme Court Building.

Over the centuries many have compared this code of law to the Mosaic law code, written much later but with similar content. But these groundbreaking laws, even while etched in stele—upright standing stone pillars—were considered a moral model and in fact, non-binding. The ideal lawgiver of Babylon was paving a path for modern law practices.

What, however, *was* legally binding were the ruler's clean-slate proclamations, called *mīšarum*.[8] These proclamations erased debts, largely back taxes owed to the government and crop rents that farmers owed to landowners for agricultural use. Based on archeological artifacts, we know of four distinct times Hammurabi proclaimed an economic clean slate.[9] In Babylonian tradition a new ruler would ascend to the throne and proclaim *mīšarum*, and in the second year it would be memorialized in a foundation stone laid in the temple. This foundation stone from 1792 BCE has been excavated, a testament to that first royal edict and the initial act of debt cancellation.

Hammurabi announced another clean-slate proclamation on the occasion of his thirtieth anniversary sitting on the throne. This anniversary edict doubled as an end-of-the-war cancellation of debts, helping the people recover from the economic losses that grew due to wartime. Then we have evidence of two additional times he canceled debts, proclaiming *mīšarum* when the economy was again in duress. As a skilled ruler, he knew that economic equilibrium on a mass scale was needed to prevent further chaos in Babylon. For him, *mīšarum* allowed for both celebration and recalibration in his kingdom. He used both law and clean-slate mechanisms to keep his kingdom intact for the duration of his rule. Maybe

---

[8] Hudson, 131, 134.

[9] Hammurabi made clean-slate proclamations in 1792, 1780, 1771, and 1762 BCE (Hudson, 69). Hudson has more to say about Hammurabi and his debt cancellation practices throughout his book.

the clean-slate actions were more powerful and worthy of note than the law code, because those were binding, while the law code was not.[10]

∼

Growing up in the Christian tradition, I was deeply influenced by Catholic, evangelical, and mainline expressions of the faith, in turn. In seminary I studied the best of biblical scholarship and filled my personal library with volumes on jubilee, biblical economics, and relevant commentaries. For decades I've been an ardent student of jubilee. Yet only later did I learn that conversations about jubilee didn't begin within the four corners of the biblical texts. Vibrant explorations of economic practice predated Moses and Isaiah, the priestly tradition and the prophetic writings. As a matter of fact, those conversation partners in scripture were actually pulling threads from their own regional neighbors. In reality, the biblical writers and early Hebrew leaders and prophets were extending the dialogue around debt and economic management from cultures and lands around them into their own context. So, like many, when I explored the jubilee passages in scripture, I didn't realize I was privy to a much longer and entailed conversation across civilizations and lands.

Knowing this now has allowed me to reframe my own understanding of the Hebrew Bible as it relates to Burundi and our development experience there. All this time I was under the impression that the jubilee texts revealed the mind of God for a just economy. But what I now know is the multiple-millennia conversation around debt cancellation and related economic tools reflects a long-lived human story of survival and sustainability. A conversation in which, according to the Jewish people, God also participated. From the depth of humanity's experience comes part of our endeavor

---

[10] How the West remembers Hammurabi for his law code and not his debt amnesty echoes our thinking of justice as punitive and not economic.

toward a balanced economic life and the practice of justice. This is our human tradition, and debt cancellation might just be one of our better endeavors that we've hidden away under the dust of history.

In rereading the origin stories in the Book of Genesis, I see the opening salvo of the book reveals a grand flourishing and a proposed purpose for humanity to be fruitful, multiply, and tend creation. In the opening narrative there is mention of God giving the seeds for every plant and seeds for every tree. And one can imagine the seeds for not only creation, but for civilizations, being given to us to fulfill the purpose of cultivating and tending the earth well. Our human purpose of tending creation, including civilizations, might hold the kernel, too, of growing humane economies to allow for human flourishing into our modern age.

A sense of pride fills me as I realize our economic explorations are part of an ongoing human conversation carried out across centuries. This is human wrestling, problem solving, justice, and ingenuity at work. These conversations and practices reflect the ongoing goodness of our creation, minds at work to address economic life as part of our original mandate.

∽

Within the history of jubilee one last artifact deserves mention here: the Rosetta Stone. Discovered over two hundred years ago in Egypt, this trilingual decree cracked the code of ancient Egyptian hieroglyphics. But what was so important was that it was written and repeated in three different languages.

The Rosetta Stone memorialized a debt amnesty in 197 BCE. It was the edict by King Ptolemy V Epiphanes announcing a debt amnesty for the kingdom. This, in a sense, provides a bookend around the jubilee canon in scripture written by priests and prophets in the seventh and eighth centuries BCE. From artifacts of 2400 BCE Sumer, followed by those from 1972–1762 BCE in Babylon that predate our biblical jubilee canon, the ensuing Rosetta Stone[11] caps a long history of jubilary practices.

What the evidence shows us is that debt cancellation was widely practiced before and after the writing of the texts of Leviticus, Deuteronomy, and Isaiah. And debt cancellation was the common practice, not a biblical anomaly. It was likely practiced in the Kingdom of Israel and Judah as well as Sumer and Assyria. What the biblical text does reveal, though, is a theological rational for how Israel viewed debt cancellation. The texts also indicate there was no need to prove the economics of jubilee, as it would have been recognizable as the default understanding of the writers, leaders, economists, and lay people at the time.

Did debt cancellation really happen? This oft-asked question about the biblical texts and the viability of the concept of jubilee reemerges. And now that question should be put to rest. What we can say with confidence is while the jubilee canon of scripture tells us about the practice of debt cancellation, the history of the Ancient Near East shows us that it was practiced—and how—in varieties of ways across various civilizations. Together, the records and text make resoundingly clear the answer to the question of receipts. Even so, they indicate another question: How can that ancient economic practice that is deep in our bones through millennia of human life and civilization be practiced today?

∼

Those who have studied jubilee have often failed to look further back in human history, back to the Bronze Age and Early Iron Age. There we see debt cancellation at work. And while the practice and receipts predate the jubilee conversation of the

---

[11] There is much more evidence of debt amnesties across the Ancient Near East, more variations on this economic theme. Those listed here are just the ones I mention in this chapter.

Bible, they are all of a piece and point to the beginning of a more comprehensive jubilee conversation across civilizations.

Jubilee practices took place across time across different lands and were called by different names by different people and much earlier than we imagined. But having the receipts of jubilary practice as part of our earliest endeavors to create a humane economy in which everyone could flourish, or at least survive, brings jubilee to the fore for its potential importance for humane economics now.

In my years of biblical study about jubilee, I thought I was uncovering what *God* believed about debt and economies. But what I witnessed early on, without understanding, was the building of the ongoing work of discovering what humans believed about debt, economies, and a just world from their various vantage points along the human timeline.

At first the revelation was disorienting for me because new data revealed the continued strands of conversation as well as how biblical writers, priests, and prophets joined the fray as they, too, imagined what better societies could look like. While the ideas that funded their jubilee canon did not originate with them or their God, they engaged the deeply human project of the growing seed of the creation story—and civilization as part of it. They brought their own fresh insight and innovation to the familiar economic enterprise, something I celebrate as I reorient that part of my tradition and study.

Some have been skeptical, dismissive of the economics of early dynastic civilizations as though they lacked complexity and were hopelessly primitive and impractical. But as Claude and I talk about the very real economics of communities in Burundi with practitioners across the globe, I am learning to see those ancient economic exploits—especially around debt forgiveness—in a fresh light. Our ancestors were deeply aware of the desired contours for a good society. At their best, they worked for a deeply humane economy.

We have failed to give them ample credit for their true civility, their humane and humanizing aims. It does no good to romanticize the challenges of our earliest relatives in their historical contexts, but I want to acknowledge the practical, generative goodness where I see it at play. Humans have been managing our economic life as a vital part of our invitation to life and creation's design. Embracing the good work of our ancestors now gets me, and gets Claude, to be part of that good, moving that work forward in current conversations and practice.

∼

Because conversations around debt are, in essence, part of the human condition, it is no surprise we see it in our first human records and in our holy texts. And it is no surprise that conversations around debt management remain relevant for our current economic woes, foreign and domestic. But it is important to know that debt cancellation is not merely metaphor or some utopian aspiration; it has always been a tangible tool on hand, as early human archives reveal how debt was an evergreen economic factor—and debt cancellation a ready tool to recalibrate the economy for the good of the realm and its people.

Because we do not see widespread debts canceled in modern economies, we assume that not only did it never happen, but that it could never happen. But we are learning the systems we live in, where people are trapped in ongoing cycles of indebtedness keeping them in permanent poverty, were not always the way of civilization, of citizenry in societies. Before Classic Greece and before Rome's roads and power structures, entire civilizations practiced debt amnesties to calibrate economies.

And those recalibrations worked.

This is the soil of biblical jubilee: ancient civilizations that wrote off debts to balance economies and survive hard times. And not only debt cancellation, but also the development of laws around land tenure and the release of debt slaves as part of the early economic practices allowing farmers, regular citizens, and military coming home from war to remain viable. This became the dust that also covered the Mosaic and Prophetic traditions as they fashioned the biblical jubilee canon familiar to traditions of the People of the Book.

~

Looking again at the Burundian word *kazoza,* which means "good future" in the Kirundi language, we hear echoes across cultures and time with other words that carry similar ethos. It is akin to *shalom* in Hebrew, the idea of communal well-being and peaceable living. This is what our economic work in Burundi has been about from its inception. And it works in tandem with jubilee economics.

The day after the marketplace fire, as Claude and the team of Kazoza Bank sat with the women behind the bank, they knew their mandate was to live up to the name *kazoza*. Their work would be to bring about a good future for all our members affected by the fire, especially the mamas desperate to provide and care for children and families.

Even without the receipts from the Ancient Near East that only came to us later, at the time we understood jubilee to be real. We knew economic justice mattered, particularly now as the ashes of the central market still lingered in the air, surrounding the women who recently started businesses, the mamas who lost everything.

Now we would join our ancestors in the economic trial and error to bring some economic renewal. We would listen to the people, the priests, and the prophets for the words they told us as though foreseeing this moment—that this was holy work. And as we listened, we stepped deep into the human mandate of humane economics in the right here, right now.

2

Jubilee Canon

Biblical economics first caught my attention as I read about the brickyards of Egypt. Deprived of their livelihood, then their land, and finally their own labor and liberty, the Hebrews embodied loss that cried out for divine intervention. They endured exploitation and enslavement, both with economic consequence. They were a people who personified scarcity. And what was the response from their god? A physical salvation and exit from the hard labor of the brickyards and deliverance that had them dancing across the Red Sea with Miriam and Moses.

The Exodus story tells of a literal liberation from economic deprivation. Maybe it so captivated me because I knew people who cried out like the Hebrews, people who were suffering under daily exploitation. These people lived in modern-day Burundi, but their life circumstances echoed the brickyards of Egypt. They fit the description of those often called the "have-nots." And they were certainly in line for some liberation.

When I arrived in Burundi for the first time, the extreme poverty shook me. Adobe-mud homes with dirt floors, street children and mothers begging throughout the city, dilapidated buildings, and nearly every paved road littered with potholes. So many of the people I met up-country had hollowed cheeks, dull complexions, and bodies thinned by malnourishment. This was the landscape Claude knew intimately. Extreme poverty was his lived experience. I did not imagine he could be shocked by anyone's impoverished state.

But the first time Claude visited the displaced and marginalized Batwa community just north of his neighborhood, he was confronted with a shocking level of poverty—even by Burundian standards. The Batwa are the third and smallest tribe in the country. Hunters and gatherers who lived in the forest until the civil war dawned, the rebels pushed them out and dispossessed them of their land. Ever since, Batwa families often cluster together on the rough edges of society. They have worked for landowners known to treat them like slaves in terms of both living conditions and compensation.

Etienne, a Batwa elder, escorted Claude to visit some of his kin living in a makeshift camp clinging to a cliff above a busy roadway. The families mustered all their energy to welcome him with dancing, a few women drumming on empty fuel cans and plastic basins. One woman squatted by a misshapen pot over the fire; she opened it to reveal a few potatoes. This was not enough for one family, let alone the several that resided in the village.

As Claude sat next to the leader, he asked his name. In Burundian culture a name reveals much about the circumstance of your birth and the hopes for your future. "Ntazina," he responded—"no name." When he was born his father thought it wasn't worth the energy required to discern his name or prospects; his mother had no hope for his future. His name and circumstances rattled Claude.

As the Batwa families gathered near Claude that day, they shared details about their lives, about living like animals, about not being seen as human by others. Later, Batwa friends would describe to Claude their lives as enslaved people; without land or freedom, which in Burundi are synonymous, they struggled to survive.

Never before had Claude encountered such poverty or precarity, which is saying something since he grew up on less than a dollar a day in the thick of extreme poverty himself. One of thirteen children, Claude watched as his dad—a pastor—would be paid with a chicken or handful of mangos, seldom enough to meet all the family's needs. He recalls many skipped meals so his younger sisters could eat. It would be years before I realized his family teetered on the verge of malnourishment throughout most his childhood.

Claude's own experience of extreme poverty made him determined to find a way out. But it was while visiting that first Batwa village that he determined to do something to break the cycle of incessant impoverishment for these families and the most vulnerable communities in Burundi.

∼

Growing up in the United States, I remember the regularity of sermons centered on tithing, and doing so cheerfully. We, the faithful, were encouraged to give 10 percent of our income to support the mission of our local church, which included funding missionaries abroad, charities at home, and the cost of running the church. Like many, this was the most prominent economic message we heard in the Bible-centered churches of our youth. A distant second were the admonitions around fiscal responsibility in our personal finances. Financial workshops in churches throughout the United States instructed people to use various envelopes of cash to help manage their spending, follow their strict program of paying down debts, as well as other "biblical" guidelines for managing household money. And the bonus if we could get out of debt, or avoid it altogether? We'd have more to give to the church—cheerfully!

Early on I learned that money, as far as the Bible supposedly was concerned, circled around the capacity to support the church. I, however, never was a very good tither, with one exception. There was a long stretch of years when I was a church leader and thus required by the pastor to tithe. Beyond that, I did not find the call to tithe compelling, with its circularity of supporting the church and its mission.

Contrast that to the quickening when I first learned about jubilee, a practice for economic renewal embedded within the Bible. Immediately I felt the transformational potential. In Egypt's liberation story I recognized something very different, something I wanted to dive into, an economic program I truly longed to practice. This is where my learning about jubilee, and my commitment to liberation theology, began in earnest.

As I studied the history and the biblical texts, I discovered that the cornerstone of jubilee was debt cancellation. On the dawn of the fiftieth year when the shofar blew, debts were forgiven, breaking the cycle of indebtedness across the land. Families were set free from the weight of debt. Communities received large-scale release; the economy experienced a reprieve. The entire economy underwent a reset. And a liberated landscape meant a fresh start for everyone.

From the first encounter, jubilee sounded expansive compared to the insular nature of tithing. According to Deuteronomy, Leviticus, and Isaiah, what I call the jubilee canon, jubilee was presented as an economic program not only about ecclesiastical sustainability but for the viability of the whole economy rooted in deep neighborliness. Releasing debt on such a massive scale allowed fiscal recovery and possibility for every neighbor and neighborhood. That one idea alone set my imagination spinning like a whirling dervish when it came to biblical economics. That scripture offered practical wisdom about something as fundamental as debt only increased my admiration for this ancient text, revealing its true relevance even to a modern context.

Even in those early days of jubilary awareness, I knew it wasn't all good news. When one person's debts are canceled, there stands another person on the other end of that promissory note. There stands someone with something to lose or relinquish to make that debt release possible. In truth, jubilee was both good news and hard news; good news for the poor and hard news for the well-off or burgeoning creditor class. Jubilee was also an opportunity for the more affluent to contribute to the well-being of their neighbors and the neighborhoods they shared together.

Perhaps this is why the American church has preferred to speak more of tithing and less, if at all, about jubilee when it comes to economics. One directs funds to the church; the other releases debts and deeds for those struggling at the bottom of the economic ladder. One leads people to believe if they give with regularity, they are in good stead with the church. The other announces that in God's kingdom, all you have is not irrevocably yours.

Jubilee requires relinquishment, breaking cycles of indebtedness for your neighbor and yourself, as well as considering your economic power as a tool either for or against the empire.

∼

After the Hebrew people arrived on the other side of the Red Sea, they began a forty-year journey unlearning the pharaonic pedagogy of their former oppression. They leaned into God's provision, mostly manna and water, amid the arid desert terrain. Nourished by a shared vision of a future land flowing with milk and honey, they came to the end of their forty years of wandering. According to the biblical narrative, they arrived at the cusp of the promised land. And they paused. It was time to reflect on the nomadic decades past and to plan for the task of settlement ahead. This is the context for the Book of Deuteronomy, an extended sermon that included a template for the new society to be forged in the promised land.

Here we encounter the first strains of jubilee embedded in the conversations around sabbath. Talk of debt release, emancipation, and hints of gleaning are featured in Deuteronomy 15, which begins, "Every seventh year you shall grant a remission of debts." And when this is practiced, Moses says, there will be none in need among the community, and there will be a strong national economy. Debt cancellation is seen as a useful tool in calibrating the economy and preventing poverty. Likely this was a lesson easily learned as the Hebrews observed neighboring nations that already practiced debt forgiveness. What held a newness to them was the regularity of the practice outlined in this text alongside the practice being initiated by that calendar rather than by decree of a king.

Within jubilee is the idea of release carried through to people enslaved: "If a member of your community, whether a Hebrew man or a Hebrew woman, is sold to you and works for you six years, in the seventh year you shall set that person free." The instruction adds, "You shall not send them out empty handed. Provide for them liberally out of your flock, your threshing floor, and your winepress, thus giving them some of the bounty with which the Lord your God has blessed you." The rational given? "Remember that you were a slave in the land of Egypt, and the Lord your God redeemed you."[1] And so in jubilee we return to Egypt and the logic of liberation. Jubilee insight, for those Hebrews in the promised land, details that freedom must be in full view and regularly practiced.

In the new land there ought to be cycles of release for those burdened by debt and for those so deeply in debt that they've become enslaved to creditors. Not only the people—even the land is entitled to a year of rest after six years of production.[2] According to the vision attributed to Moses, creation and creatures alike deserve deliverance on a regular basis to embody the spirit of liberation God intended. The echoes of this instruction go as far back as Genesis. God created for six days and rested on the seventh. In this way this cycle of seven weaves together wisdom from both the creation and liberation narratives in the Hebrew canon.

∼

---

[1] Deuteronomy 15:12, 13, 15.
[2] This is pulled from the Covenant Code in Exodus 20:22—23:33. The specific comment on gleaning is found in Exodus 23:10.

Beyond those teachings, a larger purview of Deuteronomy 15 is for neighborliness in the new land. At the edge of entering the land, Moses exhibits concern about what might undermine the ability of this generation to hold fast to its self-understanding as neighbors. And debt arises as a likely culprit. Debt not only shapes economies, but relationships. And what Moses impressed upon those gathered was that debt cannot become divisive—or definitive.

Whether a have or a have-not, a creditor or debtor, *all* are members of the community and share the same liberative history. All remember emancipation from Egypt, the hammering quotas of Pharaoh, and his economy that cost them sons, leaving too many mothers bereft. But they left the brickyards together, survived the desert together, are entering the land together—and must rise to the challenge of creating a new society together.

The construction of a neighborly economy would be imperative not only for economic well-being, but to their identity as the people devoted to YHWH. Freedom from perpetual indebtedness, a permanent poverty class, and a predatory economy would be significant marks distinguishing the emerging Israel from other nations. Their fidelity to YHWH would be showcased in their daily management of debt and commitment to their neighbors.

∼

In light of the call of jubilee and the identity of people devoted to the justice of YHWH, the American commitment to the tithe that is expected by the church falls short. Claude asks, "Is that all? Ten percent?" In his understanding the true measure of a Christian and jubilary ethic of giving is not a percentage of one's income given to the church but rather determined by how generously we respond to our neighbors.

In Burundi the institutions are often weak, lacking sufficient capacity to help the populous or offer a reliable safety net. So it is the family member, the neighbor, the fellow church-goer that comes to aid when there is a health crisis, an eviction, a shortfall making it hard to bring food to the table. You see your neighbors' need and give what you can to help. You contribute to help build their home, to cover funeral costs, to pay their transport to the village to visit family. For years Claude has covered all the costs related to his nieces and nephews schooling—tuition fees, uniforms, and books and supplies for every term. As one of thirteen, his commitment is no small amount but ensures that his siblings' children can stay in school.

I remember joining Claude on errands one hot afternoon in Bujumbura. We pulled into a parking lot, and there was an older man sitting against a tree, hunched over in the heat. I watched in the rearview mirror as Claude approached him and chatted. This was not uncommon, so I thought little of it. After he finished his errand, we stopped at a nearby pharmacy. He got back in the car with two inhalers. We circled back to the man under the tree. Claude rolled down the window and handed him the medication, and we were on our way.

"What just happened?" I asked. Then came the story. Claude has asthma. One day he went to the pharmacy to get an inhaler, an absolute must in the hot, humid, and dusty city. He noticed the man leaning on the building near the entrance, a familiar fixture around the city. He learned that he, too, had asthma. And so from then on, when Claude bought his own inhaler, he got a second one for the man. When he would see him sitting on a stoop or under a tree, he'd open the glove box of the car for the inhaler and pass it off to him. This had been going on for years. "I had not seen him in a long time," Claude said. "I wondered if he had passed on. But when I saw him this morning he was coughing. I knew he was overdue for an inhaler." "What's his name?" I asked. Claude didn't know. "Just a neighbor in need of an inhaler." That was all my husband needed to know to decide to provide his medication for years, no strings attached. Most of the time he does know the name of those he helps, but it is not required.

"If you are only giving 10 percent," Claude says, "you just are not paying attention to those around you. And you are not nearly as generous as Jesus expected his disciples to be in their life." These snapshots of Claude in action are part of how Claude sees living into an ethic of jubilee that is wedded to neighborliness in scripture. For him, it's important to reach out to people, assist in their tangible needs. Sometimes it is small but regular help, like an inhaler or school fees. Sometimes it's delivering bags of fortified porridge to a family he knows is running short on funds to feed their children. Sometimes it's helping someone find a job, get a leg up. Sometimes it's practicing jubilee so neighbors are helped in the moment and can pay it forward when they're able.

Once, as we were reviewing our finances together, I asked him what he estimates we give out to others in a given year. Scratching out some numbers on a piece of paper, he said we likely contributed about 40 percent of our income that year to our family and neighbors. Where a tithe is often a rigid act of giving that benefits a church or institution, Claude sees the call of jubilee and Jesus's generosity as for those around us, the neighbor. To him, this is the difference between a tithe and the largess of a jubilee practitioner. Jubilee is connected to neighborliness, recognizing the humanity of others and our interconnectedness, which includes economic action on behalf of one another. When we love our neighbors as we love ourselves, something Jesus commanded, we must care for their economic well-being as we would our own.[3]

～

As per the biblical telling of the economics of the people led by Moses in the desert, the lesson continued. Moses offered

---

[3] Matthew 22:37; Mark 12:30–31. Both passages pull from Leviticus 19:18. All say to love your neighbor as you love yourself.

still more detail on the laws to be codified for the Hebrews.[4] In the Tent of Meeting the people gathered for more instructions about the society they were to construct in keeping with their covenant to both God and neighbor. It is under this canopy we hear direct teaching about jubilee, the concrete economic policy of the Hebrew community.

"You shall count off seven weeks of years, seven times seven years, so that the period of seven weeks of years gives forty-nine years. Then you shall have the trumpet sounded loud. . . . And you shall hallow the fiftieth year, and you shall proclaim liberty throughout the land to all its inhabitants. . . . It shall be jubilee for you."[5] This jubilee directive is given after a description of six years of tending the land and its produce, culminating in the seventh year of sabbath rest for the fields and field workers alike. And then comes the crescendo of sabbath celebration—the jubilee of the fiftieth year. In that year debt, enslavement, and land dispossession were retired in favor of complete economic renewal. The text presents this as a fresh start, a hope for a stronger and restructured economy.

To proclaim liberty in the ancient world is code for debt cancellation. The first strain of jubilee is the release from debts—good news, indeed.[6] Next you are free to return to your family home—to be liberated from enslavement due to pervious indebtedness. And you return home. Even if the land was lost in the rough and tumble of previous years, you get the deed to your ancestral home back. The release and return is full bodied. The joy is complete. Families are reunited in freedom on their land with a clean slate so they can begin anew.

---

[4] This is the Holiness Code, Leviticus 25.

[5] Leviticus 25:8–10.

[6] This is cancellation of personal debt, mostly taxes owed to the crown and tithes owed to the temple in the Ancient Near Eastern practice. This is not about commercial debt. See Michael Hudson, . . . *And Forgive Us Our Debts: Lending, Foreclosure and Redemption from Bronze Age Finance to the Jubilee Year* (Islet-Verlag, 2018).

The jubilee instructions are more than just adjusting ledgers and transferring some deeds. It is even more than the celebration of the poor from indebtedness. Moses envisions debt cancellation as the gateway to a newly structured society where the wealth gap is closed and there is greater equity between neighbors. When land changes hands, when it reverts to the ancestral families, it is not just a return of a family home. It is returning the means of production—farm jobs, crop yields, livestock management, and revenues—to families previously locked out. The aperture for community leadership is widened, including more local families to share in the shaping of village life. Community priorities shift, shaped by all members engaged in the economic and landed life now reset by jubilee. This is a restructuring where neighbors are no longer in debt to one another but live and work in solidarity for the common good of their community. Deep solidarity dismantles the hierarchies of the "haves" and honors the agency of the once "have-nots," including them in the functions of community and economy. Neighborliness moves beyond mere niceties and toward liberated neighborhoods.

There is an echo from sabbath rest to jubilee celebration. First you sow, prune, and gather the produce of the field for six years, but in the seventh, you rest. The message is that the land will bear enough fruit, there will be enough produce to sustain you in that seventh year while the fields lay fallow. And as for the economy? After all that work, accumulation of debt, loss of land and livelihoods—there will be a stop to it. The economy will be pruned with debts canceled, slaves freed, and land returned to ancestral owners. And there is an unspoken sense that everyone is to trust that the economy will, likewise, produce ample growth to support all the families across the land.

Again, this text describes the way this community will be arranged. It is not setting out to provide receipts for how it was once carried out. Because there were traditions across the region where this was practiced in different ways, and that evidence indicates that not only was this practiced in surrounding lands and cultures, this was practiced in the promised land as well.

∽

After forty years of desert wandering, forty years of detoxing from the pharaonic economic mindset, what would liberation look like in a new land? Now the Hebrew community was about to enter into Canaanite territory. And Canaanites were known for their unscrupulous trade practices and their predatory economy.[7] Did they, in fact, walk off the economic toxicity in the desert years? Or would they enter the promised land and succumb to the pull of imperial economic thinking once again, even if this time they were not the slaves but rather the masters? Guided by the instruction of Moses found in Deuteronomy and Leviticus, the community is given a new kind of economic logic connected to its fidelity to YHWH.

They could pull from their own experience in Egypt. They could also learn lessons from their regional neighbors, who periodically practiced debt cancellation, emancipation of slaves, and land redistribution. These practices were now familiar to the Hebrews. These tried-and-true practices were used by the Sumerians, Babylonians, and Assyrians, among others, to manage their economies.

Around them they saw a primary challenge was debt management. Moses was realistic enough to know that it was merely a matter of time before this became an issue in their emerging economy too. But perhaps if they understood debt in connection with their faith tradition, connected it to their memories of enslavement and emancipation, he could help them shape a better economy.

So while jubilee practices are not technically new on the economic landscape, significant innovations to the practices

---

[7] Walter Brueggemann, *Money and Possessions: Interpretation—Resources for the Use of Scripture in the Church* (Westminster John Knox Press, 2016).

appear in scripture. Perhaps the most notable is that in the jubilee canon the practice of debt cancellation is no longer a function of the crown. It is not only on the ascension of a king to the throne that justice is proclaimed. It is not only at the ruler's discretion—when the royal seeks to recalibrate an economy in need—that clean-slate policies are decreed. Because while there were benevolent, attentive, and wise leaders who managed economies well, there were as many who were less attuned. There reigned rulers who allowed more space for creditors to rise or allowed the poor to languish longer in poverty than a more just leader might permit. So taking the proclamation of debt forgiveness out of royal hands and attaching it instead to the calendar removed a degree of precarity. Now *all* inhabitants would know when the year of God's favor was arriving—with economic relief on its wings.

Another significant difference regarding the jubilee canon found in scripture is that debt management is given a sacred rationale. In essence, how the community negotiates debt reflects its capacity for true neighborliness. This becomes a metric of love that their god observes. And when people try to circumvent jubilee imperatives regarding debt forgiveness, slave release, or land return in this community, they are called out and corrected. Even priests are expected to obey jubilee dictates (though in due course they do create some "carve outs" that will be called into question by the community).[8]

But the connection of debt release and so on speaks to another dynamic not often named. The regularity of debt-management practices is in sync with the reality of the economy. Economies ebb and flow. There are years of bumper crops and bounty, and years the locust consumes, leaving little to take to market. Natural disasters come. Wars come. New technologies come. And tools to manage the economy must be at the ready.

---

[8] Hillel, an influential Second Temple rabbi, instituted *prosbul* as a way to weaken the jubilee demands on creditors. Some say it was innovative, allowing loans to continue to flow to the poor and protect the creditors at the same time. See Jacob Milgrom, *Leviticus: A Book of Ritual and Ethics* (Augsburg Fortress, 2004).

And if they are on a regular cycle, all the better, because this speaks to the reality that economies are not static, and debt is a perpetual matter that slows economies and crushes families.

As sure as the sun will rise, debt will accrue at a rate that outpaces the capacity for repayment. Having in place a release valve for that debt that kicks in automatically is genius. It is also paired with reality.

Some talk of jubilee as an antiquated practice for ancient economies. And they add to that the notation that these texts, and the policies they outline, are utopian ideals. Far from it, what the jubilary canon reveals is an uncanny awareness about the undulations of the economy, the role of debt in that unevenness, and therefore the need for better policies in place to address the inevitable indebtedness. Not utopian at all, it is a highly functional structure. Jubilee practices were enacted—a testament to a true grasp of the economic realities in the world. Debt happens—so too must jubilee if neighbors are to live viable lives. To think that the economy will just magically calibrate itself, that its benefits will naturally trickle down to those at the bottom of the pyramid, is magical thinking, a false ideal that world economies now hold to. And not at all in sync with how economies are actually structured.[9]

~

When Jerusalem fell to Babylon in 587 BCE, the elites were taken into captivity. Exiled from their homeland for a generation or more, they lamented their many losses. They mourned the destruction of their holy city, the temple, and the world as they once knew it. Now consigned to live on the edges of an empire, the once-elite most likely existed at the bottom rungs of the Babylonian economy. Even as Babylon experienced an

---

[9] Those who lived through "Reaganomics" and the seasons since know that wealth does not trickle down, lifting all boats. It was a utopian hope that never materialized. The rich got richer, and the poor sank deeper into poverty.

economic boom at the time, the exiled were not privy to any of the benefits. These families experienced life at it was for the poor and outcasts of their beloved Jerusalem, with the added sting of exile.

It is possible to suffer deep trauma and learn all the wrong lessons.[10] You can learn that next time you will not be weak and succumb to the aggressor. Or you can emerge more empathetic, more tuned into humanity, more able to consider other ways of organizing the world to prevent such trauma to befall others in the future. Is this, I wonder, a bit of what happened when the descendants of those elite exiles finally returned to Jerusalem? Did they return somewhat chastened, willing to engage in different conversations about the ordering of the economy and society?

When their exile ended, and the Persian king allowed the Jewish people to return to Jerusalem to repair the walls, the conversations began in earnest. How would they reconstruct the city? Would they resurrect the city as it was before and hope to regain their previous status? Would they consider other options for a new kind of city?

Into the fray of repatriation, the prophet Isaiah spoke. He dared to dream of a new city, one with justice as the cornerstone. And remember, justice was economic justice; it was about equity and fiscal viability for all the inhabitants of the city. He imagined a city where the Mosaic imperatives would be embraced in full—including debt cancellation, emancipation, and land restored to each family. The horn would blow, and the jubilee would begin. It would be considered the year of the Lord's favor, indeed. A collective calibration, renewing the economic life of the city for the benefit of all.

---

[10] Speaking of the survivors of the Holocaust, TaNehisi Coates pointed out that some learned about human dignity, compassion, and nonviolence from their experience in the camps. But others learned a different lesson entirely—that next time they needed to have the guns, to be able to fight back with dominating force. "Ta-Nehisi Coates, Rashid Khalil & Michelle Alexander in Conversation about Palestine," Union Seminary, November 1, 2023.

Jubilee practice was the economic fulcrum for the new city, according to the prophet. A well-ordered economy was integral to the future viability of families, both those returning and those who had remained.

Imagine the upheaval as the exiles returned—the city walls were in ruins, yet people had remained in the wake of the Babylonian conquest. They watched the best and brightest—builders, leaders, architects, artisans—and the richest carted off in chains. And those who remained dug deep and survived. Maybe some finally held their land. And now the returnees are back, and the work of sorting out family lands stirs up old grievances and new possibilities. Would the last be first? Would the returning families reclaim land and reenter the local economy? These years must have been relieving, joyous—and fraught.

Isaiah's voice was needed. He offered a clarion call to imagine another way forward in the new city they can all build together for their mutual benefit. His was not the only voice in the raucous conversation; there were no doubt other advocacies. Some wanted to cling to the status quo, others lobbied for the "good old days" that were good for them. And those like the prophets wanted something different. As Isaiah said, the former things have passed away and God is doing a new thing among you! A new city for a renewed people—let that set your imagination, he sounded off with prophetic verve.

And so this concrete economic practice laid out in the Mosaic tradition, with roots in the Exodus, became part of Jewish law, invigorated by Isaiah as the people returned from exile years later. For generations jubilee had nourished the Jewish community, funding conversations about the best way to organize an economy and sustain families into a better future. But with Isaiah it found its wings and took flight, not only concrete economic practice but as a metaphor for deep transformation and a wider equity for all. Jubilee unfurled into a vision of favor, of what it looked like when God's favor shone across the land.

3

Jubilee Campaign

Claude recently returned from a tour of East African countries, hunting for hope and signs of lived jubilee. What he witnessed sparked a small measure of optimism. He found it in Kampala, Uganda, where a young man who survived life as a street kid now fed street kids in the slums. He found it in a man in Kenya who gathered AIDS widows, women living with the disease long after their husbands were buried, and offered them compassion, community, and, when funds allowed, medication. These practitioners functioned on the fringe of their Christian congregations, as their pastors and priests labeled them crazy radicals, disowning them from the mission of the church. Yet this was the locus of hope Claude experienced during his travels. People like Caleb and Edward made a difference in the material life of the communities where they labored with deep love.

What was clear to Claude was not only how each was disconnected from his local church, but how profoundly they were misunderstood by the leadership and marginalized by faith communities. They worked in near isolation. But he knew they were not, in fact, alone. Claude decided to gather them, and others like them. Maybe in meeting one another they could discover their commonality, offer encouragement, allow for commiseration, and find fresh resources for their various works. This space would be called Amahoro Africa, and our first gathering was held in Uganda in 2007.

I remember sitting with Claude in our stateside living room, deciding together on a theme for his keynote address to the practitioners he anticipated meeting in Kampala. We looked at different gospel texts. When I read from Luke 4, the first sermon Jesus preached, Claude leaned back and closed his eyes. "Read it again," he said.

> "The Spirit of the Lord is upon me, because he has anointed me to bring good news to the poor . . . release to the captives . . . to proclaim the year of the Lord's favor."[1]

As we continued talking, I noted that the year of the Lord's favor is also called the jubilee year. It is the cancellation of debts, the release of those enslaved due to indebtedness, and the return of ancestral land to families that lost them in the rough and tumble of the economy. I added that Jesus pulls the thread from the prophet Isaiah's dream for the new city, Jerusalem rising from the ruins.[2]

"That describes my hope for Africa, to rise from years of ruin with a dream and a strategy," Claude said.

I read the text again and the verses that followed where, after Jesus read from the Isaiah scroll, he said, "Today this scripture has been fulfilled in your hearing."

"So," Claude said, "Jesus was inaugurating a season of debt forgiveness for the poor. And said it started that very day? Then

---

[1] Luke 4:18–19, 21.

[2] Jesus reads from Isaiah 61:1–2. He stops reading before the text turns toward mention of "the day of vengeance of our God." He was, it seems, interpreting in real time. Additional vengeance was not necessary for those already under the heavy domination of the Roman Empire. And perhaps Jesus was following in the footsteps of his mother, who sang of divine reversals of the social order without a spirit of vindictiveness or violence. For further comment, see Kelley Nikondeha, *First Advent in Palestine: Reversals, Resistance, and the Ongoing Complexity of Hope* (Broadleaf Books, 2022), 68–69.

this is for us, now!" The immediacy of jubilee animated him. "This is the word for African practitioners—today we begin living into jubilee in our communities."

Claude and I understood jubilee at the time as both literal and symbolic. We grasped that what Jesus advocated was a tangible release for those hemmed in by debt, sickness, heartbreak, and other consequences of oppression. According to Luke's telling, Jesus was surrounded by fellow Galileans, many of whom were local fishermen barely eking out a living in the small fishing village where the synagogue was located. These were the impoverished ones of society.

Jesus and his neighbors lived under the weight of the Roman imperial yoke. They labored to survive in a rapidly changing economy, one that moved away from periodic debt cancellation practices and land return, and instead indulging the burgeoning creditor class that Hebrew priests and prophets railed against.[3] Their ancestors could count on the arrival of the jubilee year to experience some measure of return and relief. But not so under Rome. As the economy undulated under occupation, people struggled to forge new strategies to survive the economic violence. All this was compounded by the well-known Roman military cruelty. And in that moment in time Jesus looked into their eyes and proclaimed jubilee.

"There is no better news for a poor person than to tell them that their debts are forgiven," Claude said. He recalled his own uncles. They always owed people. There was no other way to survive on the bottom rungs of the Burundian economy but to take a loan from one neighbor, another from a family member, still another from a cousin up-country, and maybe an additional one from your employer in the form of an advance. The reality for most people he knew was cycling through these debts ad nauseam, treading water to just subsist.

---

[3] Michael Hudson, . . . *And Forgive Us Our Debts: Lending, Foreclosure and Redemption from Bronze Age Finance to the Jubilee Year* (Islet-Verlag, 2018), 17.

Almost everyone needed loans. The announcement that all your debts, all at once, were being canceled? That would be good news for Claude's neighbors, uncles, and for most Africans working to survive in precarious economies today.

What seemed clear to us was that Jesus understood the plight of his neighbors amid the hardship of the first-century economy. He meant what he said literally—today we should reclaim the concrete economic practice of jubilee and all it entails regarding indebtedness, enslavement, and land seizure. So, then, we surmised, transformative works must be tangible. Our work must address the actual struggles of people, not merely spiritualize them. Feeding street kids mattered. Assisting AIDS widows with medicine and other forms of care mattered. All was deeply faithful work. These tangible works were akin to jubilee. These acts made a material difference in the lives of these women, children, and men. This kind of freedom was what Jesus intended his gospel to do.

And jubilee, in the hands of a poet like Isaiah, also offered metaphoric velocity. The year of the Lord's favor was also *like* jubilee, when all debt accrued in the past is canceled at once. It is *like* the restoration of all that the locust have eaten. It is *like* the Spirit doing a new thing after successive empires repeated the same violence. It is like emancipation from Pharaoh after hard service in his brickyards. It is the kind of large-scale renewal that transforms our lives into goodness we only imagined.

Claude and I believed that the jubilee campaign Jesus proclaimed in the synagogue addressed actual circumstances of his oppressed community *and* their aspirations for the unfettered largess that the prophet conveyed when he imagined the year of the Lord's favor. There was a need to take the poverty of his neighbors seriously—and jubilary conversations did just that. Those discussions likely sparked the agency of his followers to begin living into this new reality where they could begin to break cycles of indebtedness, even if their debts would not be written off in full by rich creditors. They could step into jubilee values by forgiving the small debt their neighbor owed them, offering restitution when possible, and reclaiming neighbor care as resistance to economic entrapment. Talk of jubilee in the shadow of the imperial economy reminded people that there was another economic program on offer, another way forward was possible.

And this practical, metaphoric, and restorative jubilee is what Claude wanted for Burundi, and for Africa. This jubilee is what I wanted for all my neighbors. Because it meant a better economy that truly would lift all boats, but so much more than that.

∼

There is a cliff hanger at the end of this passage written by Luke. Jesus reads from the Isaiah scroll and announces jubilee. He is then asked to do in his hometown what he did up the road in Capernaum—heal people. But he refused to be coerced into performing signs and wonders. At his refusal, it is said, they drove him out of town and attempted to push him off the cliff. In the simplest sense of the story, I accepted that the events recorded their rage at wanting a healing that was not on offer and feeling slighted.

But there is another possible explanation. The accepted practice throughout the region had been periodic debt cancellation and related actions to offer relief to those trapped in debt and to restart the economy. This all changed drastically under Rome. The rise of oligarchs was significantly aided by Caesar allowing creditors to bankrupt debtors, enslave them in perpetuity, and foreclose and seize their land. And there was no debt cancellation on the horizon. As a matter of fact, any word about clean slate initiatives were heard as uprise and ended with death. Records from the time reveal numbers of people killed for advocating for debt forgiveness.⁴ Under Roman occupation, it became a dangerous proposition.

And so I read this story about Jesus publicly preaching jubilee and advocating for debt cancellation to begin immediately against this Roman backdrop of violence. Maybe the people were enraged that healing wasn't on tap that day in Nazareth. But more likely the religious leaders feared local Roman functionaries would catch wind of the words spoken in their synagogue and come down with a heavy fist. Likely some in the religious establishment were in league with the Romans, not unlike the tax collectors, finding ways to benefit from the new economic system. They, then, may have been trying to protect their financial gains, or were anxious to keep the social peace in their town. But they certainly knew Jesus demanding debt cancellation could disrupt everything they worked to preserve. So perhaps they angled for him to be threatened within an inch of his life.⁵ They let the crowd push him to the edge of the cliff to send a message, not about healing but about dangerous talk about debts. And if he did get pushed to his death—well, they would have done Rome's work and been rewarded, not punished.

People with vested interests in the Temple's status quo or the "new normal" emerging under Rome would have seen any proposed jubilee campaign among the poor as too volatile. Something to be shut down.

In first-century Palestine, talk of debt cancellation was perilous. People died speaking those words. Yet regardless of the risk, Jesus declared jubilee. Imagine an economic policy that made an empire shudder. That's what we have in our hands with the practice of jubilee.

---

⁴ Hudson, 223. Hudson notes that by the first century CE the idea of debt cancellation was becoming a utopian notion. But even before that, in the first century BCE, "Roman aristocrats killed populist leaders advocating protection for debtors and land redistribution."

⁵ One might recall the crowd that turned on Jesus during Holy Week, swayed from shouts of "Hosanna!" to "Give us Barabbas." Crowds are easily manipulated.

While Claude noticed the immediacy of jubilee on the lips of Jesus that morning in Nazareth, my attention was arrested by something else. Jubilee is good news for the poor but hard news for the well-off. On the other side of those canceled bank notes and IOUs were other families. Land deeds returned to one family meant another handed them over and waived its claim. Jubilee was hard news for those with power, requiring relinquishment by the well-off. But this is what economic renewal demanded: both relinquishment and return. This is how equity would flourish so every family had a chance to thrive, good harvest or bad.

This is why we ought not be surprised that those with vested interests in the economic system tried to find a way around debt-cancellation policies of sabbath and jubilee. Hillel the Elder, an influential Jewish religious leader, wrestled with jubilee in the decades before Jesus. He posited a policy called *prosbul* to create a work-around for those who saw the jubilee year on the near horizon and thought twice about lending money to a neighbor or acquiring land that soon would be returned to the original owner when the horn blew. According to this policy of *prosbul*, creditors required their clients to waive their rights to enjoy debt cancellation in the coming jubilee year. If this was done in advance of the jubilee before Temple functionaries, then the transaction was not subject to jubilee release. On the face of it, this seems like an obvious weakening of the jubilary intent of Moses as well as the priests and prophets who followed him.[6]

However, some translators, like renowned Jewish scholar Jacob Milgrom, believe that *prosbul* was actually a creative mechanism to preserve economic equilibrium while honoring the jubilee year.[7] *Prosbul* solved one problem for those in need

---

[6] Hudson, 9, 145.

[7] Jacob Milgrom, *Leviticus: A Book of Ritual and Ethics* (Augsburg Fortress, 2004), 303.

of a loan, allowing them to borrow any time necessary, since the policy allowed creditors to remain open to such transactions even as the jubilee year neared. It solved another problem for the creditors, protecting their acquisitions, especially land, even in the shadow of jubilee. According to some, the practice was both practical and innovative.[8]

Hillel saw *prosbul* as part of Jewish practices for "the repair of the world" as well as the maintaining of the social order. Regarded as an insightful thinker and leader, he may have held that this was in keeping with the best of Jewish thought and practice and that it somehow synced with Moses and the prophets. But it also revealed just how much influence of Roman economics had on all loans to be repaid, jubilee or not. Finding creative ways to circumvent sabbath and jubilee imperatives regarding debt cancellation may have been less innovative than evasive, less faithful to the ethics of the new city.[9]

∽

These might have been among the conversations that Jesus, a good rabbi, engaged in with his disciples as they walked the dusty roads of Galilee and beyond. Certainly someone who read from the Isaiah scroll about the economic tradition of debt cancellation and declared it a contemporary practice would have fielded many subsequent questions. How do we properly enact it? How is it even possible while under Roman domination? How does *prosbul* factor in? We are not privy to those exchanges in a direct way. But that does not mean we are without resources when it comes to knowing what Jesus thought about *prosbul*.

Consider another conversation between Jesus and his band of followers that we are invited into by the Gospels.[10] When they ask him how to pray, the good rabbi offers a model prayer. In

---

[8] Julius H. Greenstone, "*Prosbul*," *The Jewish Encyclopedia*, 219–20.
[9] Solomon Schechter and Wilhelm Bacher, "Hillel" (the general entry about him and his teachings), *The Jewish Encyclopedia*, 397–400.
[10] The Lord's Prayer is found in both Matthew 6:9–14 and Luke 11:1–4.

it he instructs them to pray that their debts would be forgiven, as they forgive the debts owed to them. It is stunning to have this economic line in the middle of a prayer template, but that is Jesus, upending all our expectations both then and now.

Under the Galilean sun Jesus taught his disciples to pray about their most tangible concerns—bread for today, no debts for tomorrow, and the end of violence forevermore.[11] The structure of the prayer itself followed an ancient rubric regarding the worries of the poor. Even under Rome's heavy hand, the hope of the have-nots was for ample food for their families and debt relief on the horizon. The matters that pressed upon the population most were central to Jesus.

In this context, even without knowledge of the original language or an exegesis of the exact words used, it is clear that the conversation is about concrete things—food, debt, violence. It is not a prayer about forgiving sins and releasing hard feelings, as I once was taught by those taking the prayer out of context.

I first learned the Lord's Prayer in a catechism class. It was rote memorization of the perfect prayer, "Forgive us our sins as we forgive those who sin against us." As I grew up in church and circled back to the prayer, I was told that we were praying for our sins, our bad behavior, our sins of commission and omission, to be forgiven by God. We prayed that we would be able to forgive those who have sinned against us, who hurt us with mean words or gossip, anyone who harmed us. Maybe my understanding of the prayer corresponded to my own social location in a middle-class family. I never thought to pray for food on the table or the cancellation of family debt. It made

---

[11] John Dominic Crossan, *The Greatest Prayer: Rediscovering the Revolutionary Message of the Lord's Prayer* (Harper One, 2010), 182. Crossan shares an example of the ancient zeitgeist from the second century CE, two reliefs in the Roman Senate House from the time of the Emperor Trajan. One shows Trajan distributing food to a woman with a baby. The twin relief shows a line of people carrying debt tablets to the emperor to be burned. It is bread and debt, paired together. It was the hope of the downtrodden (140).

sense to pray about behavior, not something as real as daily bread. But my context dimmed the straightforward meaning of the prayer for too many years.

Over years of translation, the meaning of the words regarding debt have shifted in the direction of the more spiritual, transgressions or sins.[12] I was not alone in this interpretation. We pray this prayer without a single thought given to actual debts that we carry. That, we assume, is a conversation to have with our bank or other creditors. Yet the weight of indebtedness, then and now, is at the heart of this prayer for the faithful. Release from debt is so essential to human well-being that we ought not be surprised to find it on the lips of Jesus, one who shared in the all-too-human condition of poverty.

The prayer Jesus offered his disciples ushered them into the economic work of debt remission in real time. They did not need to wait for this empire, or a subsequent one, to proclaim justice in order for their debts to fall away. As they began to pray this revolutionary prayer day after day, their worldview could shift toward a jubilee-centered reality. And as their sight line changed, so could their own practice. Debt forgiveness in this landscape would begin with the disciples releasing their neighbors from debts owed to them, and vice versa. Releasing one another from debts would begin breaking the cycle of indebtedness that plagued them all.

Maybe a disciple's prayer for debts to be forgiven would be first answered when a neighbor cancels the debt owed him. Maybe the first surge of economic freedom would happen at a microlevel, among neighbors refusing to accept debt as necessary. Neighborliness meant, among other things, not ensnaring your neighbor into debt.

This prayer encourages a subversive grassroots approach to economic renewal, all in keeping with the spirit of jubilee that

---

[12] Crossan's book is a good resource for better understanding the history of translation concerning the prayer. Hudson, . . . *And Forgive Us Our Debts* is an academic and more current treatment of the history and conversation around debt, including this prayer and its translation.

Jesus previously announced in a synagogue in Nazareth. So when Jesus said jubilee begins today, it was not an unrealistic ideal. He intended it to begin with his disciples. Breaking the wheel would start with those with the least structural power as they reached for tools from other nations, and other times. Jesus empowered his followers to enact jubilee now—no need to wait for a king's proclamation or the sound of the shofar. Jubilee was now put firmly in the hands of the people to practice whenever necessary. Jesus's declaration was one more jubilary innovation.

The Lord's Prayer, with its tangible economic language and intent, has also been called the Jubilee Prayer,[13] as indeed, a prayer than encapsulates the jubilee spirit, where debts are a serious matter worthy of daily prayer and reimagined practice to break cycles of indebtedness on all levels of society. Imagine if all of us who know this prayer by heart took the challenge embedded in it seriously? It would start a groundswell of jubilary motion and economic reform. But that would only be the start, as we still need the systemic reform of the economy at large to truly set everyone free. But this revolutionary prayer is a place to begin, now, wherever you are, whoever you are, in the larger movement of jubilee.

This prayer taught by Jesus to his friends and neighbors also serves as a commentary on *prosbul*. We should practice debt remission as often as we can. This is the opposite of trying to swerve around the jubilee imperatives to protect your recently acquired land or waive your right to debt release to get a much-needed loan to survive. With the largess of jubilee we are called to be releasing one another from debt as often as we can, and giving generously when possible to help others survive in times of hardship. Hillel's innovation to help creditors keep land is not nearly as adjacent to jubilee as the Lord's Prayer that Jesus gifted us.

---

[13] For a connection of the Lord's Prayer to Isaiah 61:1–2, hearing the intertextual jubilee connection, see Sharon H. Ringe, *Jesus, Liberation, and the Biblical Jubilee* (Wipf and Stock, 2004), 83.

The cornerstone of Claude's keynote address at the close of the Amahoro Africa Gathering was Jesus launching his jubilee campaign. He spoke to African and Western friends, a mix of practitioners and theologians gathered together to dream about hope for Africa. The kind of tangible transformation these African practitioners sought in their various communities corresponded to the call for real debt remission in Nazareth and across Galilee. Whether it was fighting food insecurity, offering healthcare, or social work in the red-light district, all these works were as concrete as dropping debt. The jubilee campaign rang out like a siren call around the room. Some felt relief at the good news of debt forgiveness and confirmation of their ongoing prayer for it. Others inhaled the words like a new energy source for their efforts, work that was faithful to Jesus even if their church leaders did not understand it. Many in the room felt the forceful jab of jubilee, its challenge to relinquish what does not belong to you.

The room buzzed with electricity, Claude later recalled. People started giving money, though there was no collection. Then some who collected the funds together decided to use them to help those fellow practitioners they knew were in need. They had listened to one another during the conference, and now were able to direct resources wisely and generously. Around the room conversations about new partnerships happened. Jubilee stirred them all to action in a scene that must have been reminiscent of the synagogue in Nazareth that day of Jesus's declaration of jubilee.

One outcome from this initial season of jubilary study for both Claude and me was a reflection on our own personal practice. All those small, and some not so small, loans we'd given out over the years—what should we do? Claude came to an answer more quickly—of course we forgive the debts. And then we decided together that when at all possible, we would make gifts instead of loans. We would give without expecting anything in return or entrapping people into more debt. And for the most part, we've been able to live up to the jubilee imperative embedded in the prayer we still say in our family.

Another outcome of the jubilary words for us was embarking on a community development project in Burundi with thirty Batwa families. These women and men brought their children to a pristine plot of land in Matara, a region up-country where the sky is blue, the soil red, and the land covered in shades of vibrant green. It was a chance to begin anew after seasons of living like enslaved people elsewhere. And from the very beginning of the project we held jubilee conversations.

I remember a few years into the enterprise learning about an initiative around livestock. Each family would be given two pigs. The hope was the families would breed pigs, good for meat and lard at the local market as well as fertilizer for their crops. And more pigs would mean more money, as litters multiplied over time. It seemed like a good investment for the community.

Word traveled to Claude that the Batwa leaders decided, with the approval of all the families, that each family would give its second litter to a family in a neighboring village. This would not directly enhance the economic growth of our community, but slow it down. But their desire to offer a tangible blessing to their neighboring families, to offer them the same support they received, benefited the larger community.[14] They realized that their neighbors' flourishing added to their own. There was no need to hoard resources—even pigs. So they took their litters and shared, allowing nearby villages to benefit from the piglets they were initially gifted.

This was jubilee in action. And jubilee practices engender more jubilary practices. It was not our idea. It emerged from families' own experience of abundance. The jubilee seed grew in them, and what emerged was generosity toward their neighbors.

---

[14] Our work, Communities of Hope, is a partnership with Mark and Laura Shook of Community of Faith Church in Houston. Together we worked with our Batwa friends to bring about a new landscape for them.

The jubilary signature of their commitment to share goodness with others, to contribute to the economy for more than just themselves, exceeded my highest hopes. Our Batwa friends demonstrated, yet again, that jubilee is not only a concrete practice, but also a dynamic that refuses to be limited by literalism to only loans, labor, and land. Sometimes it is the gift of a litter of pigs that incarnates the jubilee spirit.

Jesus engaged in another set of jubilee conversations that we often miss. The Gospel of Luke records the story of a rich ruler who approached Jesus with a question, "Good Teacher, what must I do to inherit eternal life?"[15] Jesus pointed him to an abbreviated recitation of the Ten Commandments, a Jewish standard for measuring goodness. The command prohibiting stealing is particularly related to the matter at hand. Amid the economic turbulence of the times, to be called rich likely meant you cheated the system somehow, stole property that belonged to another family, through *prosbul* perhaps, or otherwise colluded with the exploitative imperial power to gain financial benefits. It might have been legal or common practice, but in the eyes of the Good Teacher it was stealing.

The rich ruler insisted that he had obeyed all the commands since his youth. So Jesus homes in on one thing the ruler lacks. "Sell all that you own and distribute the money to the poor . . . then come, follow me." Much of what the ruler owned was rightfully the inheritance of other families. And so the invitation on offer was to relinquish everything, sell and distribute, so that the money moved toward the victims of such economic machinations. Once this was done, then the man could join the jubilee campaign of Jesus.

Hearing the jubilee challenge, the rich ruler became sad. He was very rich and very unwilling to relinquish any of it.

---

[15] Luke 18:18–30.

Maybe the hardest command of all is jubilee, the one that the wealthy have tried to circumvent for centuries. Jesus noted that this is the reason it is so hard for a rich man to enter heaven.

But equally interesting is the conversation that ensued after the ruler walked away, still rich but now sullen. The people within earshot of the interaction asked, "Then who can be saved?" There was a Jewish cultural tradition that believed that God blessed good men with wealth. Job comes to mind. If a man like that, with the sign of blessings, cannot enter God's kingdom, what hope is there for anyone else? Jesus, unflummoxed, responds with the reassurance that while it might be impossible for men is possible for God. I imagine Jesus had the face of the rich ruler in the front of his mind, the man who did not accept God's help in the work of jubilee.

The story continues as Peter advocated for all the disciples, "We have left our homes and followed you." And Jesus affirms them. He knew they relinquished homes and families to join the jubilee campaign. They will get things back in this life . . . and the afterlife as well. They get a promise regarding eternal life that the rich ruler did not. And it hinged on jubilee: those who relinquish will receive a return, a reward.

These conversations display how difficult jubilee practice is for the well-off, that there is something that must be relinquished. Hard news, indeed. But for those who can let go, who can sell and distribute, the good news of jubilee is theirs. And they are part of this subversive campaign to recalibrate the economy right under the nose of the Roman Empire. Jubilee is an opportunity for the affluent to make a choice for the sake of their neighbors. By agreeing to relinquish deeds and forgive debts, they contribute to the stability of their local economy and facilitate a deep equity that is a hallmark of neighborliness.

Jubilee spoke not only to material wealth, but also power structures. Like the Roman rulers, some priests preferred the stability of a system that benefited them. And here Jesus aims one final jubilee conversation in their direction. Jesus tells a parable about Lazarus who begged outside of the gates of a rich man. The rich man daily ignored Lazarus. When the rich man died, he was subjected to torment in the afterlife. And in the afterlife it was Lazarus, the beggar, who ascended to the side of Abraham. Jesus made clear that even if someone returned from the dead to herald the importance of caring for those in need, it would not matter to the rich.[16] They had already been warned by the example of Moses and the prophets—those known to be staunch advocates of jubilee in life. The rich man, and others like him, had already received their warning from Moses, the prophets, and now Jesus. Acting on behalf of your neighbors in need, working to create structures that promote viable living for all, is central to the jubilee campaign as well as wise economic practice.

At a time when indebtedness was on the rise among his kin, but debt cancellation had fallen out of favor with the reigning imperial power, Jesus took the risk of a public declaration of his jubilee campaign. He no doubt heard news of other populists killed for advocating such policies. And he knowingly rocked the boat. But economic justice stood as a pillar of his vision for society—he could not do otherwise. Jesus carried the jubilee campaign forward into the first century and by his example has commissioned all who call themselves disciples to follow suit.

---

[16] Luke 16:19–31.

Part Two

The Practices of Jubilee

4

Loan Practices

Among the things smoldering in the ashes of the marketplace fire was—necessarily—our rigid understanding of the jubilee practice of debt cancellation. The loss of inventory, business, and savings had hit our bank members hard. Rising in its place from the still-hot economic embers was an invitation to revisit our understanding of jubilee economics with now greater complexity as we heeded the contextual realities on the ground in Burundi. As the theologian, I began with scripture. Claude brought his on-the-ground community building to begin with the women and men shifting through the ashes of their businesses in a marketplace that was, simply, gone.

In those initial days, laden with lament, calculating losses felt both necessary and premature. Through the lens of the Book of Lamentations, it looked as though there was none to offer comfort.[1] So many of the small microlending programs in Bujumbura serving a similar constituency shuttered operations in the wake of the fire. Some never opened their doors again, never offered a final conversation to their borrowers. They took what little they could salvage and left town. No

---

[1] "None to comfort" is repeated like a drumbeat throughout Lamentations. The Daughter of Zion, the personification of Jerusalem, cries out that no one is present to comfort her in the grips of her grief, no one to witness her loss.

wonder countless people felt there was no one to comfort them in their hour of need.

Claude and the Kazoza Bank team took a different approach. They held space for shared sorrow. They acknowledged the pain. And they allowed lament to shape the conditions for our next moves.

While I pored over the jubilee canon in scripture, Claude activated an outreach campaign to all our bank members who did business in the central market. Every loan officer was deployed. He instructed them to visit any Kazoza members who were hospitalized with injuries or burns sustained trying to rescue their kiosks. Sit with them, he said, listen to them, make sure they have what they need. The same was true for visits to other members: go to their homes and check on them. What do they need to survive the next set of weeks? Claude worked to get pallets of rice, beans, and cassava flour, which his team then distributed to our members so that their families had food. The only imperative: *Do not ask them about their loan.* This is not the time to ask if they can repay the loan. This is the time to listen to their pain, address whatever needs you can, and assure them we are in this together.

While his team crisscrossed the city on hospital visits, house calls, and food deliveries, Claude worked on another part of his jubilee plan: securing capital to extend loans and to make payroll for our staff. Our partners in Houston responded by wiring a generous gift to Burundi immediately. They understood that this was not the time to retreat or withdraw resources, but rather to double down on the economic potential of the Kazoza Bank's mission and members.

With funds secured, Claude asked all the members affected by the fire to make an appointment with their loan officer. He tasked each officer to determine what members needed to get back to work—an extension on their repayment horizon? an adjustment on their interest rate? additional money added to their loan? Create a plan based on their needs, he said, to get them back into the economy, one by one.

Next came the matter that would require more creativity: assisting the mothers. The women that met Claude that Monday morning were the most precarious of our members. In banking terms, they fell into the category of high-risk borrowers. They had little or no previous business experience. They had no collateral. They had no physical address, no location where their business could reliably be found. This made it impossible to secure funding elsewhere.

But the mothers had worked with Kazoza for many months building up their small businesses. And the fire incinerated everything they had to show for their efforts. While we could not legally erase their debts, we refused to walk away from them. After weeping together, Claude was determined they'd dance together on the other side of all this—if it was possible. Kazoza's work to survive absolutely had to include them in the redemption story, the story named jubilee.

Claude enlisted the help of his community. He had many well-off friends in town. They were generous within their family systems, as is Burundian tradition. But he compelled them to practice a greater generosity on behalf of these women, to see them as members of a shared community and worthy of their support at this critical juncture. So together with five such friends they formed an association called Uburundi Bwacu (Our Burundi) in quick order.

They immediately started planning a fund-raising event on behalf of these women. They reached out to their friends and secured a hotel venue, invited local artisans and fashion designers to participate. The guest list was a "who's who" of Bujumbura—including representatives from embassies, nonprofit organizations, and other institutions. They put on a dinner with music and showcased the latest Burundian fashions on the runway. And they featured the stories of our Kazoza women, inviting several to share their experiences of loss and concern regarding their ability to provide for their families now.

Centering the stories of these women cut through any pretense that might have lingered among the crowd of those with means. Their truth telling, singed by the fire, thick with grief, was an appeal to a deep humanity; the women spoke and invited a solidarity not often seen in Burundi. "Our Burundi includes us," they testified. Their tears galvanized those gathered to see them as part of their family, and to give accordingly. That night the association raised over $50,000.

The raised monies established a guarantee fund for the women. This became their collateral, allowing each mother to extend her loan and renegotiate the terms of repayment. The balance of the fund and the interest that the fund generated was used to offer the women technical support for the coming months. This included various training sessions, individual coaching, carpenters and materials to rebuild kiosks in other small markets, and more. Kazoza assisted 1,280 women with that guarantee fund, with ample funds to also include 400 women from other local institutions. The fund helped a total of 1,680 women stay in the economy.

The idea was to leverage that fund to make reentry as easy as possible for the mothers. It also allowed us to facilitate their reentry into the economy without canceling the debt, thus keeping our banking certificate. A creative solution in the spirit of jubilee.

Watching Claude, the Kazoza Bank team, and friends who created Our Burundi, I began to see the jubilee texts from scripture anew. At its deepest and widest, jubilee practice mandated reentry into the economy after a hard season. No one should be locked out of the economy—or consigned to poverty permanently. Participation in the economy should always be on offer so that families can live and even thrive.

In the ancient economies debt cancellation across the board accomplished an economic reset for the population. The priests and prophets of Israel understood this and adopted the practice in their land. Debt forgiveness allowed people another chance to enter the economy after the locusts, after a famine, after a war or other catastrophic loss. These were real debts canceled. And that pushes us to consider releasing such debts whenever possible. But when we can't, our work is not done. Jubilee practitioners remain committed to creating pathways back into the economy. We lean in with determination and creativity. Jubilee economics does not allow debt to pull people into a downward spiral or keep them trapped in vulnerable conditions.

Those three months after the central market fire transformed our practice of jubilee. We pushed beyond a rigid reading of the jubilee canon into a more open and generous understanding. Interrupting incessant cycles of loss, letting people back into the economy, and freeing neighbors from endless poverty now form our definition of jubilee. Yes, we cancel debts when possible. But jubilee offers a broader responsiveness to the economic needs of our community, requiring us to do whatever we reasonably can to keep people in the economy so they can make a viable life for their families.

The jubilee canon mentions the imperative to set people free from debt and debt-related slavery, and to send them off with resources to start again.[2] This points to the importance of the reentry arc. "Do not send them away empty handed," Moses instructs in Deuteronomy. Give people what they need to start over, some measure of capital to begin again. Otherwise, they return home without the means to recover from years out of the economy. They remain functionally locked out of the economy, a condition the text makes clear is not ideal.

Full emancipation includes the means to reenter the economy so freed persons can start providing for themselves and their family as before. Those who free them must give from their resources; they are responsible to make reentry possible from their own wealth. There is a thread of reparation in this call to make freedom complete. But the spotlight is

---

[2] Deuteronomy 15:12–14 speaks of setting a slave free and sending the person home with provisions from your flock, threshing floor, and winepress. So send them with livestock, grain, and wine.

on the actions necessary for economic viability on the other side of enslavement.

I realized how crucial entering the economy was to jubilee. What bars people from entry? Debt. Enslavement. Land loss. And the jubilary texts address these very things—because each is an impediment to the economic viability that families need to survive. So we must negotiate these dynamics, and obstacles like them in more modern and complex economies, as jubilee practitioners. If some reality stands between people and their ability to work and earn a living, then we ought to be addressing it with all the jubilary energy possible.

After weeks of work by the entire Kazoza Bank team, the members gathered for a meeting to discuss the progress made. All the loan officers had renegotiated loan plans for members affected by the fire. All the mothers, the most high-risk borrowers, were able to stay afloat. Additional economic rescue allowed a number of women from other institutions to get needed assistance to stay in business. Our people were back in business!

Then the manager of membership spoke up. She reported that Kazoza added 800 new members in the month after the fire. While everyone else was working with our borrowers to recover, the neighbors were watching. They saw that our doors remained open amid crisis. They noticed that we visited our members in the hospital and made food deliveries. They heard stories from members about recovery plans. And they decided that is the kind of bank they wanted to be a part of, too. The staff reported this in shock. We thought we might be on the brink of closing, but instead we grew.

We found our purpose as a financial institution in the weeks after the central market fire. Jubilee economics acted as a cornerstone. Our widening understanding of those practices allowed us to discover that creating pathways to prosperity was the core of jubilee content—and our core commitment. We pledged to keep economic entry points open and support the business enterprises of our neighbors in the spirit of jubilee.

∼

It was in this time that as a theologian I watched the scripture expand. Our literal embrace of jubilee and the charge to cancel debts aligned with the desire to take the text seriously. When the bottom fell out of our young financial institution, an institution started to serve the working poor and grow their economic capacity, we asked ourselves: Do we hold fast to scripture—or our commitment to our Burundian neighbors? Were those at odds? What emerged in the collaboration between Claude and me was a way to remain steadfast to both as our understanding of jubilary action expanded.

∼

Three years later Claude and I landed in Uganda to attend a conference held by our friend and church pastor Moses Mukisa. The annual event centered on the theme of transformation, and Moses invited Claude to offer a keynote address based on our work in Burundi and the community development theology that underpinned it.

Claude spoke of the loss, lament, hope, and hard work that formed our approach to transformative work in our communities. In the Q&A session that followed, the emcee facilitated an extended period of time for questions. People were so curious about the place of lament in community development and wanted to hear more about how Claude defined hope in such tangible terms.

After the session a woman approached Claude and introduced herself; she was a fellow Burundian and former member of Kazoza Bank. She wanted to thank him for making a way for her to survive the central market fire.

The time after the session was a bit rushed, with a breakout session to host with practitioners in an adjacent room, so Claude invited her to join us. As we began our conversation about the nuts and bolts of our work, Claude changed the agenda. He ceded the floor to her, asking her to share her own story in full with the group. She stood proud in front of us and told us that she had a good business and was finally able to put her children through school in Bujumbura. The future was looking up. And then the fire in the market that Sunday morning robbed her of her future. She was among those who wept with Claude the following morning. She said that at the time she could not imagine how she'd manage to rebuild her small business. But she was among the beneficiaries of the guarantee fund. She was given a fresh start, and she took it. Now her business is expanding to Kampala! Her kids are happily in school, and she just bought a small car. She claimed that good future, *kazoza*, for her family.

I don't know how much her testimony meant to the practitioners gathered that morning. But Claude and I kept dabbing our wet eyes. She had entered the economy again and stood as a testament to jubilee thriving. Once she sat down, we hosted a conversation about development work. One man raised his hand and asked if crying together made the women more loyal to our institution, as if our tears were a calculated tactic. What the shared tears point to is our willingness to enter the pain with others and let it inform our response to the loss, Claude pointed out. What emerges is rooted in reality, often shaped by the spirit. It is not a tactic, but a pattern we experienced with the central market fire and other losses across our years of community development work.

Woven into our jubilee sensibilities is an awareness of the loss and our willingness to be in proximity to the pain, allowing ourselves to be in relationship with the bereft and share the deep ache of loss. We cannot rush to reenter the economy. We must feel the pain and make it part of the fabric of the new garment, the new hope on the other side of loss.

∾

"Jubilee is expensive," Claude said over our morning coffee recently. "Tell me more," I said. He explained the reality of running a bank, now that Kazoza Bank has celebrated its

Loan Practices

ten-year anniversary, and how costly it is to practice jubilee in modern economies. A bank is a business. It needs to make money in order to loan money to members. Some of the money traditionally is made in various fees that bank members pay to maintain an account or take out a loan.

But from the beginning Claude designed Kazoza with the 97 percent of Burundi's unbanked in view, creating a low threshold for entry into our bank. Given his familiarity with those living in extreme poverty, he knew why most never opened a bank account. They could neither afford the minimum amount required to open an account nor maintain the monthly minimum. They certainly could not afford the additional fees charged each month by banks. So, as Claude recalled what his mother did, they put their money in empty Nido cans and hid them in their home or buried them in the garden. It wasn't a secure way to keep their savings, but at least there were no fees eating away at the little they managed to stash away.

So Claude began Kazoza Bank with a policy that made it easy for people like his own parents, aunts, and cousins to open an account. All they needed was an identity card—no money necessary to enter the banking system. Kazoza also did not charge monthly service fees on accounts. And there was no fee to get a bank statement (in this region it is expected that you pay for a banking statement, since it was not online). This zero-zero-zero policy made banking accessible in a new way for those in his community. Now there was a secure place for their savings, they could have a checking account, they could take advantage of direct deposit if their company offered it. They could also begin forming a relationship with their banker, moving toward opportunities to participate in a microloan program or apply for a loan. This was no small thing for aspiring business people who needed access to capital.

Another part of the Kazoza origin story is the creation of a hybrid banking model that combined elements of microlending and community banking. It took nearly a year for the Burundian Central Bank to approve this new model. The microlending model allowed a wide entry point for those interested in starting a business. They could join the program and learn basics in the training sessions while connecting to other women and men starting out. They had access to loan officers, likely for the first time in their life. They began with small loans, building both their business and the financial muscles needed to run it. The team paid close attention to these entrepreneurs and their business progress.

The truth that Claude had learned from microlending in the past is that small loans are inadequate to fuel a true business enterprise. In order to maintain certification from the Central Bank, microlenders cannot lend more than a few hundred dollars to any one borrower, thus the prefix *micro*. But those who really have the knack for growing a business will quickly outpace the microlending threshold and need more capital to grow. Sadly, a commercial bank will not even take a meeting with a potential client without the client possessing more than $10,000 in collateral. So there is this huge gap between $300 and $10,000 to overcome. It is impossible.

Claude created a bank model that solved that gap. Those women and men who had the mind for business and a good product or service, who rose quickly to the top of the microlending pyramid, were invited to meet with a loan officer and discuss a proper loan. The loan would be an amount that suited the enterprise they were building, and part of the loan requirement included ongoing training. The entrepreneurs would have access to a banker who knew them and their work. There were trainings that were specific to their industry (food and beverage, textiles, agriculture, and so on) and business skills (basic accounting, planning, staff management), tools in our business center like computers and free wifi. Such insfrastructure was an additional expense, but critical to facilitate the growth for our members. Even the trainers we hired presented ongoing cost, but we knew they equipped our members with new skills and connections. We determined these expenses were worthwhile for the jubilee project at hand.

Years before the idea for Kazoza Bank was formed, our network of African thinkers and practitioners, Amahoro Africa, was growing into a larger conversation across several countries and multiple years. Our fourth annual gathering convened in Kenya, on the edge of the Indian Ocean in Mombasa. The theme this particular year was Gospel Economics. I offered the opening keynote lecture, intended to launch conversations for the day around the idea of living as a jubilee practitioner. I spoke of the Patriarch Joseph, who became the food czar in Egypt, managing the empire through a season of food insecurity that ended with his own kin enslaved to Pharoah. Joseph was a good man in many respects, but it turned out he was a poor economic practitioner. I contrasted him with Jesus, a jubilee practitioner who invited his disciples to do likewise in both prayer and praxis. My point was that well-intentioned people can miss the point when it comes to economics, mindlessly obeying the status quo rather than opting into the jubilee campaign that can transform a neighborhood.

The lecture sparked spirited conversations around lunch tables, during tea time, and into the dinner hour. Many friends fiercely defended Joseph. So our evening session included an impromptu panel for them to make their case, furthering our conversation. They spoke of his innovative grain silos, how he made the food supply last, and his obvious leadership abilities helping him rise to such a position. My final word? When Joseph was on his deathbed, he implored them to take his bones with them when his kin were at last free. . . . I believe he knew that he contributed to their enslavement and felt its weight. He, too, wanted to be liberated. I then asked if we could all agree that ethical economic practice should not land our neighbors in slavery, or the modern equivalent.

This set of conversations functioned like good seed tossed into the soil of Claude's heart. This, he recalls, prepared him for the opportunity to start a bank when the opportunity landed in his lap a couple years later. Could he create a banking model that would address the economic needs of his neighbors and align with the jubilee campaign of Jesus? Could a bank be a mechanism for jubilary action?

And that's when Claude began to realize, from experience, that jubilee is expensive to enact. As other financial institutions in Bujumbura make their bottom line by charging those fees for opening accounts, maintaining accounts, and providing statements upon request, he knew jubilee called for something different and, to date, Kazoza Bank has resisted following suit.

We remain determined to make entry into the economy as accessible as possible in the spirit of jubilee. But Kazoza pays for its jubilee commitments. In a fragile economy it is hard to forgo the fiscal buffer that those fees provide when your bank needs to remain viable. But our model makes a priority of easy entry. It is over the long-term relationship with our members, as they take out loans and hire people and use more of our banking services, that they pay into the institution. And that will keep the threshold for entry affordable for the next batch of members wanting to start on their path to prosperity.

However, over the past set of years commercial banks who once shunned the unbanked and mocked Kazoza Bank for offering them loans are now changing their tune. They have seen that there is a burgeoning capacity in our members, and they are looking for growth in their numbers to appease their shareholders. These commercial operations are now starting to target our members right at the time they secure collateral and start paying into the Kazoza model, offering them attractive terms that they can afford to extend given the considerable size of their regional banks.

We are glad to see our members given real opportunity and banking options, something they never had before. We are glad the banks finally see them as attractive borrowers with increasing potential. We understand that our members need to go where the best terms are available to them. And yet, it makes our model less sustainable. It makes it harder to hold to the jubilee-centered commitment of no fees upon entry and minimal fees in the early part of the banking relationship. We don't want to change our zero-zero-zero fee structure, but the cost to Kazoza Bank is real and, in the future, might force our hand. This is not only part of the cost, but part of the trial and error of jubilee practice in the modern economic landscape.

Our small bank, now serving 80,000 Burundians in our twelve branches, has survived a fire and grown ever since. We suffered losses and lamented them. We leaned into creativity. We moved forward with hope and hard work. We made entry (and reentry) as easy as possible. We've seen members come to us for their first-ever banking experience, and years later they are taking out $25,000 loans for their successful businesses. We've watched our members put children through school, build homes, create jobs, and help others start businesses. We know what jubilee looks like in real time. But we are aware that for all that good news for our members, it does often cost Kazoza Bank, which also tracks with the hard truth of jubilee. Our relinquishment of greater profits is part of creating the conditions for economic viability for our neighbors. True jubilee is thick with good—and hard—news.

∽

During the holiday season of 2019 I heard Trinity United Church of Christ in Chicago forgave millions of dollars in medical debt for its community. Even before I knew the details, the jubilee connection was clear. At the time, medical debt saddled two out of five Americans, affecting their credit score, their ability to secure housing, and even jobs that require credit checks.[3] Rev. Traci Blackmon, the associate general minister for justice and local church ministries of the United Church of Christ, and Rev. Otis Moss III, the

---

[3] Krysten Crawford, "Study Finds Medical Debt Relief Doesn't Always Work," Sanford Institute for Economic Policy Research (April 2024).

senior pastor of Trinity UCC in Chicago, worked with local congregations and the organization UNDUE Medical Debt to make this jubilary action a reality.[4] The churches bought the medical debt of their most indebted neighbors in Cook County, purchasing the debt for pennies on the dollar. They were able to wipe out $5.3 million dollars of medical debt by raising $38,000.

The church-goers emptied the change from their pockets or bottom of their purses into the donation basket. Many of them carried debts of their own. But they gave what little they could spare to participate in a biblical kind of generosity toward their neighbors. That glimpse of deep solidarity with their neighbors captivated me and cracked open yet another layer of jubilary comprehension: jubilee practices are relational, and they strengthen the neighborhood.

Recipients of this jubilary gift received yellow envelopes in the mail just ahead of Thanksgiving wishing them happy holidays and telling them their debts had been forgiven. This was a blessing to their neighbors in Cook County, not based on church attendance or faith or any other factor beyond their human need for relief from the burden of indebtedness. This clean slate came with another benefit—the medical debt was erased from their credit report. This meant that their credit scores immediately improved, opening the door to beneficiaries for new opportunities when it came to applying for housing or seeking a loan or submitting to a credit check for a job.[5] Real debts were canceled; tangible benefits followed in quick succession. This is jubilee in the modern world.

The work of UNDUE Medical Debt addresses the weight of indebtedness for many Americans. It deals with the actual debts—and the related extraordinary collection actions like

---

[4] UNDUE Medical Debt was previously RIP Medical Debt. For more information about its work and how to participate, see its website.

[5] Celeste Kennel-Shank, "How a Network of Chicago Churches Is Helping Erase More Than $5 Million in Medical Debt," *Faith & Leadership* (December 2019).

lawsuits, liens, and wage garnishment.[6] It ensures beneficiaries will be free to move back into the economy in the season ahead, unencumbered by a poor credit score like a millstone round their neck. Because what jubilee practitioners know is that erasing debt alone is insufficient. People must reenter the economy with resources—like a much-improved credit score—that make their life more viable.

However, even such a good initiative is complicated. A recent study conducted out of Sanford University found that the medical debt relief did not always work as hoped.[7] The research revealed that even after forgiving the medical debts that had gone to collections, the lives of beneficiaries were not necessarily bettered. Finances were still hard, credit still scarce, and even the toll on mental health still plagued them. But, the researcher was quick to note, this does not mean the efforts are unhelpful. What the study points to is the need for more work.

Intervening before debt moves to collections might offer greater long-term results. Working on the cost of healthcare and medications, including advocating for better legislation in these industries, must be part of the conversation. Addressing extraordinary collection actions that cause additional harm is another critical matter to be addressed. But the team of researchers and people at UNDUE Medical Debt all agree that this is a season of trial and error, working to find the best way to alleviate the heavy indebtedness and bring greater financial freedom for Americans. This study does not dissuade their energy toward debt forgiveness, but educates them on how to adjust the work to be most effective for fellow citizens. That is the spirit of jubilee—dedicated and creative when it comes to allowing people back into the economy.

---

[6] UNDUE Medical Debt details its ongoing policy work against extraordinary collection actions (ECAs) alongside its work to retire medical debts. It notes that many states are moving to ban the practice of medical debt affecting credit scores, but the work continues.

[7] Crawford.

Jubilee practioners are always learning and understanding ways to implement jubilee practices. For Claude and myself, that jubilary work requires action and reflection, the ability to bring creative solutions to a problem but also evaluate effectiveness and course correct as needed.

Jubilee enterprises must be as nimble as debt is complex. The news will not always and only be good, but confronting the complexities of modern debt is worthwhile work. It is justice work. So we work to cancel debt when we can, get creative in addressing debt when necessary, and always think about equipping people for reentry into economies for the benefit of their families.

5

Labor Practices

Once I witnessed a group of prisoners being released.

In Burundi, when you cannot pay your hospital bill at the end of your treatment, you are not released. You move to another ward with others who cannot pay. You are no longer a patient but a prisoner until the debt is paid in full.[1]

That day Claude and I stood outside the Prince Régent Charles Hospital, the oldest in Burundi, and watched as former patients walked out into the sunlight, finally free. A few hours earlier they were patient prisoners.

The day we entered the ward there were over forty men and women of varying ages sitting or lying on beds. Family members brought them food and news from the outside. But until someone paid their bill in full, they slept there night after night. Many had been there for months. Most had no idea how the bill would be paid. Since they could not go to work, they looked to family and friends for help. But they, too, were unable to spare enough francs to help. That ward, complete with armed guard sitting out front, was a dreary place. Whatever relief they felt once treated quickly dissipated as they languished in the makeshift prison. Hope was on lock down.

---

[1] A friend from the United States, Sarah Mays, alerted us to the plight of patient prisoners. She raised money on her college campus and asked Claude to use those funds to set as many people free as possible.

Claude listened to stories shared by a few of the prisoners, translating for me. There was a bad bout of malaria, a broken leg, a severe eye infection. . . . They fell sick, then they fell prey to debt. It happened that fast.

Armed with a better sense of the situation and a sense of jubilee purpose, Claude found the hospital administrator. They sat together with the accountant and calculated how much it would take to release all of those held in that one-room ward. He bargained—and made the case that they could be guaranteed money today or wait for months and still not see a single franc from these families. His argument won the day—and won the release of all the patient prisoners on site.

It felt as if we sat out in front of that administrative office for hours in the hot sun waiting for all the paperwork to be done. But I was not leaving before I saw each person walk out, bill paid in full and free.

Slowly, slowly, they started to walk by. Each got release papers signed, receipt stamped, and then walked out. It looked so ordinary. But we sat there and witnessed jubilee. People were being set free, as Isaiah imagined and as Jesus hoped. It was a parade without much fanfare, but laden with jubilary goodness.

I cried. Claude counted. He made sure every last person was released. Jubilee requires dreamers and bean counters.

Just a couple of years later he heard rumors of patient prisoners held at a local women's hospital, trapped because of their post-treatment debt. He decided to investigate. He found sixty-eight women in the dismal courtyard, sunken faces, despondent after months of captivity. He sat with them. He listened. Their words pierced him. He couldn't conceal his tears as he told me about their conditions. Some were dipping into depression, seeing no hope for any future. His morning plans instantly derailed as he committed to hours with these women, mourning side by side. It was December, days before Christmas.

He reached out to our partners in Texas. Could we fund the release of these women in time for them to be home for Christmas? Return to their families, to their children, would be the best gift we could give them. Our friends agreed. And so Claude negotiated with the administrators (another jubilee skill, apparently) until an agreement was brokered. All those women, most of them mothers, left the hospital with a clean slate.

Again, there was no ceremony. No pomp, nor circumstance. Claude stood in the foyer making sure each woman exited the facility. He handed each bus fare. The spirit of jubilee hung thick in the air around them as they boarded mini-buses to their homes.

It never gets old watching people set free.

~

In February 2021 the Burundian president tasked the mayor of Bujumbura with the creation of a registry of all the unemployed youth in the city, a city that represents 15 percent of the country's population. After months of surveys the registry was completed. The results were stunning. The rate of youth educated for the workforce (high school graduates, university graduates, those with a vocational certificate) that could not secure a job was 67 percent. The data paralyzed the government. Where do you start to tackle an employment gap of that magnitude?

When the data became public, Claude got to work. He began writing a training manual during his off hours at night. The thesis: in this economy, where jobs are scarce, only you know your skills, your character, your commitment to hard work. Therefore, you need to create your own job and be your own boss. His hope was to open a conversation about entrepreneurship among young people in the Burundian context. To inspire and equip them to create a job for themselves, to build a business that could allow them to hire others. Then they would strengthen families, empower communities, and yes, invigorate the economy at large.

Claude wrote a proposal to accompany his manual. If the government adopted this program, it could use it in schools and churches during the off hours for free training space. Claude offered the manual for free. All the government needed to provide were the trainers. He presented it to the mayor, who immediately saw the value of the proposal. But, he said, he had no resources to allocate to the implementation of such a plan. And that could have been the end, stymied by the data and lack of capacity to respond.

But Claude refused to stay stuck—too many families were connected to that 67 percent unemployed youth data point. This was the genesis of Kazoza FM. Claude and the Kazoza team worked on another proposal—this time to the National Communication Board of Burundi—requesting a license for radio and TV broadcasting. It took months, but finally Kazoza was granted a broadcasting license. Now there was a platform to take that economic content to the airwaves and make it available to all the youth in Bujumbura and beyond!

Kazoza FM: The Voice of Development, became a 24/7 training platform. Now people can learn how to be entrepreneurs in their local economy and find a community of people working in the same direction; 103.3 is a spot on the radio dial for tools to build a better future, a spot of hope. Claude hosted a weekly show, "Be Your Own Boss," where he hosted long-form interviews of successful Burundian entrepreneurs known to the community. There was the popular Masterclass Series, where short radio segments featured how to apply for a loan, how to apply for a business license, how to prepare for an interview, and other business essentials. All this is basic information hard to source and extremely confusing if you do not have a well-connected family member or a mentor to guide you. Kazoza FM tried to fill that gap for the youth ready to get to work.

The target demographic for our radio station is those aged eighteen to forty, those primed to enter the workforce. The station has all the usual features, too: music, sports, and talk shows. News is focused on economic news, the things happening in the city that effect the economy and the emerging entrepreneurs. And a full 30 percent of the content each day is economic education. So while people tune in to laugh and be entertained, they also get economic lessons to slowly shift their thinking and equip them when they are ready to engage.

On Kazoza FM we've hosted a comedy competition, "American Idol" style. And we have hosted a now annual singing competition that invites local artists to create the "summer song"—an original song of hope for the long, hot Burundian summer. It has become a block party, bringing young people to the streets to sing songs of hope. We believe that kind of hope sparks hard work and gives people a reason to believe that their labor can create jobs and positive change in their community.

Kazoza FM is now the number one station across the nation. That standing invites ample advertisers to make the radio a sustainable platform to deliver economic education for a new kind of economic engagement. What paralyzed the government leaders acted as a catalyst for Claude, the jubilee practitioner determined to create paths to prosperity for families. Our hope is that young people see that another way to enter the economy is possible. And this is part of jubilee—entry into the economy.

~

In the aftermath of the central market fire Claude and I learned that reentering the economy stood as a critical tenant of jubilee. In a precarious economy, external exigencies can impinge on the system at any moment, disrupting the livelihoods of good people hard at work. And beyond the loss of a job, families are in the wake of any fiscal disaster. Conversations about debt, enslavement, and property address the most frequent obstacles to economic viability. These very dynamics can thrust people out of the economy—and lock them out. So opening avenues for reentry matters. That is key to families securing the potential to thrive today and into tomorrow.

But in Burundi we learned that entering the economy at all can be fraught. Young people can do all in their power to secure a diploma, a degree, a certification of some sort, and still find they are on the outside of opportunity. When the doors to economic engagement refuse to open, it is another sort of jubilee infraction. And if jubilee is, as Claude believes, creating pathways to prosperity, then entry matters as much as reentry.

Kazoza Bank was built on the idea of identifying and empowering the burgeoning business people previously trapped at the bottom of the local economy. In retrospect, Claude intuitively knew this was a jubilary enterprise worthy of our efforts. Even before we articulated the connection between the reentry conversations witnessed in scripture to entering into the economy, we were practicing it with jubilee energy. Once we did see the connection though, our conviction compelled us to do more in the direction of making the economy more accessible to those who needed to be in, wanted to be working, and those eager to provide for their families. Such activity also contributes to the vitality of a community, which is another tangible benefit of jubilee actions.

Kazoza made bank accounts and loans available to people trying to access the economy. The addition of Kazoza FM radio made better economic education available to a younger demographic, those primed to enter the economy and begin to make their own contribution to the viability of their community. Economic information was contextualized to address the current conditions of Burundi's economy and the readiness of the youth to learn new modalities—especially entrepreneurial ones. But we also looked further afield to creating higher quality jobs, not only in our banking branches and development enterprise, but also in our fortified porridge factory.

∼

Burundi Fortified Foods came to life in 2017, when we realized that fortified porridge was an effective curative for school-age children in our elementary school who suffered from malnourishment. Fortified porridge also made massive improvements in health indicators for pregnant and lactating women in our Bubanza community. So we increased our school feeding program to include the mothers. At first we purchased porridge from a local co-op of women. But as we expanded the feeding program, we needed more porridge than they could produce. We knew we needed access to more high-quality porridge to feed not only the mothers and children in our community, but to widen our reach and help other communities battling malnourishment. And so, with the partnership of some friends, we launched a porridge factory complete with a newly outfitted factory and machines, tested (and then certified) porridge recipes, and a distribution network to get the porridge into local markets by 2019. But at the heart of Burundi Fortified Foods was our program to feed the mothers and children in vulnerable communities, which now serves over twenty-five communities.

One thing that a porridge factory needs is a variety of grains for natural fortification like wheat, corn, sorghum, soybeans, and sesame. That meant relationships with farmers. Claude decided our porridge factory would source locally grown grains. This made financial sense, since it would decrease the cost of transporting grains from Tanzania or Uganda. But he also wanted to create more economic opportunity for local farmers. In Burundi, 90 percent of the people are small scale farmers, farming to survive. These women and men have some agricultural familiarity but not ample capacity to turn a profit.

Claude drove north toward farming country, where a majority of farmers lived and worked. He spent time walking their small plots, listening to the stories they shared about their families and the hardships they endured season to season in a constant effort to survive. Farming was not easy or lucrative, but it is what they knew. He asked if they were open to expanding their farming operations in partnership with us. They responded in the affirmative.

Based on those conversations he developed a way forward that would increase economic outcomes for the farmers and bring health benefits to their families. He arranged a long-term lease of 100 hectares (about 250 acres) of prime farm land with the government. He then invited the farmers to take a plot and begin planting. We laid an irrigation system. We employed a full-time agricultural engineer to offer training and support to maximize the effort of the farmers. Each season we provided the necessary seed and fertilizer. We began with thirty farmers, but the number quickly grew. Now over four hundred farmers work an expanding number of plots to deliver crops to create our fortified porridge.

The arrangement between the farmers and our factory includes contracts for their crops in advance, giving them assurance that what they plant and harvest will be purchased for a good price. We built a collection station in their province so they did not have to travel far to deliver the grain. We pay them on time—a big deal in Burundi where farmers are often paid late. And we pay a small portion in fortified porridge for their families, so they enjoy the health benefits and see their children beat malnourishment. These farming families are part of the process, and their economic growth matters to us. Witnessing the increased viability of their families is part of the goodness of our battle against malnourishment.

∽

Woven into the fabric of economic conversations in the Hebrew Bible is the imperative to pay wages to workers in a timely manner. Moses tells those gathered, eager to enter the new land, that there will be expectations for employers. They must pay workers their daily wage before the sun sets. And this instruction applies to all their workers—whether Israelite or foreigners. Some of the other jubilee practices, like loan forgiveness and land return, have carve outs that exclude foreigners, but not here.

When it comes to compensating the workforce, the instruction is universal. You will not withhold wages, not even overnight, for any worker. Timely payment is the new rule. For those still trying to loosen themselves from the weight of generations of enslavement, you can understand the importance of respect for work and prompt payment for their labor.

Moses makes it clear that workers rely on their wages for survival. His address to the congregation also puts any aspiring employers on notice. If an employer dares to withhold wages or delay payment even for the night, that employer risks the workers crying out to God. In this context it is clear that Exodus is in view, the way the enslaved people cried out to God from the brickyards—the way God heard them and responded with emancipation.[2] Withholding wages from workers is akin to enslaving them, behaving like Pharaoh, who demanded work with no pay. The warning is clear: if employers inch toward pharaonic practices, then they best be ready to tangle with the God who emancipates slaves, punishing empires and their predatory economies.

When I first read this instruction, it hit my ears like hyperbole. In the Western context that was familiar to me, salaries were for the most part, on time. Most Westerners experienced pay for work arriving like clockwork and often direct deposited into their bank account. I understood that non-salaried workers should be paid on time, too. And that invoices should be paid on time out of respect to those workers and suppliers. So, the connection to pharaonic behavior still seemed antiquated and extreme.

This understanding shifted when I lived in Burundi, and as Claude described elements of a frustrated economy and its workers. It was in Burundi that I witnessed another economy more like the one Moses described. It is not uncommon for Burundians to work for months without pay. Often they had no idea when their employers would pay them, so they lived with daily precarity. If you or another person in your household

---

[2] Walter Brueggemann, *Deuteronomy* (Abingdon Press, 2001), 48.

did not get paid in time for the rent or for grocery money or tuition fees, then you began taking loans from your relatives or neighbors. You could find yourself owing a little to a lot of people as you tried to survive, even as you showed up to work each day.

This was the first time I realized that you could have a job but not have reliable pay. It was so cruel to witness an entire economy that could not, or in any case did not, honor paydays. Moses's insistence on prompt payment—before the sun sets—began to make more sense to me. Everyone deserves their wages on time.

Claude took the words of Moses to heart. From the day we began employing people, we paid them on time, every time. Our workers never had to watch payday come and go without pay. And over time, they learned that they could trust payday and plan their finances accordingly. Claude took a measure of pride in paying on time, doing for his workers what was seldom done for his father and other family members. He was breaking the cycle. He was obeying Moses, honoring both God and his neighbors.

Today we employ 380 people across our various enterprises. People want to work for our bank, our porridge factory, and other development projects because we have a reputation for paying on time, all the time. This is no small thing in Burundi. Yes, we pay our team well. We also offer health insurance. But you cannot underestimate how much it matters to Burundians that we pay on time every payday. It gives them assurance not afforded to most others in their economy. And watching how much our employees appreciate prompt payment makes me see how critical the words of Moses were, then and now. The sun should not set on unpaid wages to our workers.

∼

But the words of Moses were not only about unpaid wages to workers eking out a living. What he knew then, and we know now, is that delayed payment to workers can mean that the money remains in the hands of the owners. Every day the money stays in their hands, they are free to make more money on it.³ They do so at the expense of their workforce, those who often live paycheck to paycheck. Withholding pay, even for a day, is another way of robbing the poor.

Having grown up in these circumstances, Claude expressed his exasperation, like the writer of Proverbs, regarding those who stole from the poor. These were his family members and neighbors, and the rich found many ways to rob them. However, he believed that God would have the last word when it came to their ill-gotten riches.⁴

Claude knew of a program started by the World Food Program with the hope that a milking cow would offer a poor family both milk for the children and fertilizer for their fields. One of our friends in Burundi was contracted with the Burundian Ministry of Agriculture and international NGOs to secure these cows for rural families. Bosco (not his real name) would do small contracts, like bringing in one-thousand cows from Uganda for rural families.

So, in the earlier days of our community development work in Matara, Claude wanted to provide goats for the thirty Batwa families and, of course, he reached out to Bosco, knowing if he could get cows that he likely could get goats, too. He ordered ninety goats, intending to give each family three goats. But the day the goats were delivered to our friends in Matara, Claude could scarcely believe his eyes. The goats were thin and sickly. They would not last long enough to be of any benefit to the families. Claude cried.

Together he stood with Bosco as they watched the goats unloaded from the trucks. How could he in good conscious give such poor-quality goats to these families? And if this is what Bosco delivered when a *friend* placed the order, Claude wondered about the quality of the cows provided to the families he had no connection to at all. Did they last long enough to

---

³ Ibid.
⁴ Proverbs 22:22 comes to mind.

provide milk or fertilizer to the families who eagerly awaited the gift from their government? Or did the cows expire as quickly as these goats would, offering none of the intended goodness because of the contractor's greed?

As he wiped away his tears, he chided Bosco, "If you do not give these families what they deserve, God will come after everything you've earned at their expense." Bosco laughed.

Claude refused to pay for the goats, obviously. He was able to find someone else to provide healthy, robust goats to our families in Matara. But he was so disappointed to discover that a friend was profiting off the poor, treating them with such disdain, and unbothered by it.

Not long after this incident, Bosco had the opportunity to bid on a massive contract with the government for thousands of cows for more rural families. He leveraged everything—all his capital, using his three homes as collateral for huge loans, all to secure this contract. He succeeded. And he imported cows from Uganda for the many rural families desperate for some good fortune. But he met with a twist he did not anticipate: the government never paid him a penny on the contract. The poor condition of the cows was too egregious to ignore. The rural families cried out. And there was not a bribe large enough on that day to buy off the government officials.

Bosco lost everything. Exploiting the poor for personal gain landed his own family in poverty. As we heard the news, we thought of Proverbs 22:22:

> Do not rob the poor because they are poor,
>   or crush the afflicted at the gate;
> for the Lord pleads their cause
>   and despoils of life those who despoil them.

It does not always happen immediately, but sometimes scripture does come to life right before our eyes. The words of Moses also reflect this same sentiment, that a divine backlash awaits those who dare to exploit orphans, widows, or poor rural families.

At the height of the Industrial Revolution in the United States, owners of factories and railroads and the like made out like bandits. Exploitation of workers grew their wealth. Exhausted to the bone with long hours and hard labor in dangerous conditions, the workers cried out.

Their cry ushered in the union movement of the nineteenth century. Unions galvanized workers to organize and even strike for better wages, better hours, and safer working conditions. Their strategic solidarity secured an eight-hour work day, a forty-hour work week, and overtime pay. Their solidarity broke the cycle of child labor. They gained safer conditions. Some even saw health benefits and pensions. Each advance improved the livelihood of laborers and the prospects for their families and communities. Unions functioned as a jubilary vanguard on behalf of workers in a predatory economy. Their advocacy advanced imperatives aligned with Mosaic sensibilities.

Over the subsequent decades unions have waxed and waned. They have battled with various industries, monopolies, and political parties. But even so, they continue to partner with workers for a better workplace and brighter economic trajectory.

As the precarity of the economic landscape increases, cries from workers and actions by unions should come as no surprise. They hold jubilee aspirations rising to the surface of society.

Taskmasters and pharaohs alike ought to beware when God is summoned through the cry of the poor. Whenever workers cry out from their brickyards—or assembly lines, delivery trucks, or writers' rooms—they are heard. What comes next is often jubilary action to set people free from their economic chains, and what often comes after that is neighbors creating paths back into the economy for those recovering from debt, enslavement, and exploitation. And while there often is a gap between unions and the very poor, who often don't have their rights represented, it's a model that holds jubilary insight and from its origins, the roots of the cries of the working poor can be heard.

Jubilee policies and practices include conversations about how we enter, reenter, and operate within the economies in which we live. Creditors and debtors are in full view. But included in the discussions are bankers, business owners, and employers who interact with workers daily. The ethical function of these women and men can create conditions that support a viable livelihood for workers and their families. Paying fair wages—and promptly. Ensuring safe working conditions on the job and healthcare. Banking programs that are accessible to every worker. Making the economy work for our neighbors embodies the spirit of jubilee; it is neighbor love in action. And we are welcomed into a world where the lives and livelihoods of our neighbors matter and motivate us to stand up for their well-being in tangible ways.

When jubilee is our lens, economic actions matter. Do we respect the labor of our neighbors? Are we willing to curb the greed of others—and ourselves—to allow ample space for neighbors to flourish? Do we open the door to better opportunities for others and safeguard them from exploitation? Even deeper than the cry of jubilee is the call of our neighbors asking for a response worthy of their humanity, of our shared humanity.

6

Land Practices

Kibira Forest was the land of Burundian legends. Rich and varied trees created a green canopy across many miles of pristine terrain undulating with gentle slopes. A lake, waterfalls, rivers like blue ribbons coiling through the soil as part of the natural irrigation system for the rainforest. Home to all manner of flora and fauna, Kibira embodied an Edenic goodness. No wonder it became the favored hunting ground for the kings.

This lush land also was the original home for the Batwa, the Indigenous people of Burundi. In this verdant forest they hunted; they gathered. Their songs mingled with the birdsong; their feet pounded out exuberant dances on the red soil. Their pottery tradition began with clay from the heart of the forest. Batwa culture was shaped under the canopy of Kibira. In this place the Batwa were the fullest version of themselves.

But in the late 1950s international conservation groups joined with national governments to forcibly expel the Indigenous communities like the Batwa from land they newly declared for national parks and forest preserves. The forest became known as the Kibira National Park. What was a victory for the conservation movement was eviction and loss for the Batwa.

Then Burundi's civil war started. The forest became a base camp for the rebels. Once again the Batwa communities were the casualties.

Turned out from their homelands and offered neither compensation nor recourse, this was the initial injustice. The Batwa became a marginalized and displaced people in their own country.

Expelled from their land, they lost their capacity for self-sufficiency. Most were reduced to the harsh and humiliating reality of a landless existence, migrating farther away from the forest. They resorted to squatting on farmers' lands while selling their labor for food or begging for money, which reinforced their cultural position of inferiority. Ejection from the forests also meant an end to Batwa hunting practices, part of their cultural identity, and prompted a severe decline in health conditions for the tribe.

When we first connected with our Batwa friends, they were battling such conditions. They lived on the edge of land that was not theirs. Their children did not attend school due to severe discrimination. They were seldom invited to join communal events like weddings or celebrations. After our years working together in Matara, our friend Jacqueline acted out her previous existence for us during a community celebration gathering. She crouched down low to the ground, making herself small. She covered herself with a tattered piece of fabric. Then she jumped up, threw off the fabric, to reveal herself smiling and in a new dress. Because now, she said, she felt human. "Before, I was not human. I was just a slave to others." Initially, we found our friends landless, which in Burundian culture is synonymous with hopeless.

∼

I learned in Burundi among the Batwa that land was not mere property. Land was about connection to ways of life. It conferred, or denied, identity. Those who possessed a plot or place, like a forest to roam, lived tethered to a land that nourished them with food, water, but also meaning. Land was the first or primary gift to a community, conveying a basic goodness on which the rest of life could be constructed. Without it, one lived life bereft.

This was fundamentally different from my own American understanding, where ownership was desirable but not the sole indicator of meaning or sustainability. Home ownership did not determine my state of belonging; I could rent and still live well and have my rights as a citizen. I imagined finding meaning, not fortune, in teaching or nonprofit work that would keep me a renter, barring me from homeownership. But this was a choice; it was not associated with an existential hopelessness on my part. Time spent with my Burundian family and our Batwa friends opened the door for me to understand the weightiness of land possession—possessing a land that possesses and supports you—and therefore jubilee, with more clarity.

I would get another crash course in land possession (and dispossession) when I later made pilgrimages to Palestine. Ancestral land, thick with terraced olive trees, was not merely home to families. It was bone of their bone, flesh of their flesh. I was confronted with people who held land differently, more deeply, than I ever had. I witnessed a landscape with the potential for holy hospitality but also violent injustice. What happened to the land happened to the families that called it home in undeniable ways.

By comparison, my connection to the notion of land was cavalier, likely due to growing up as part of the privileged class in my own country. I could imagine having or not having land and still living a good life. Living in the patchwork of subdivisions littered with tract homes, land did not seem especially dear or determinative to me. All the parcels felt interchangeable, like Legos, so I developed a casual concept of land. My friends in Palestine had no such luxury. Land was life or death; it held hope or represented devastating loss.

These two communities taught me lessons about land I needed as I approached the jubilee canon. Land was no small matter. It had formative power. It conferred a blessing or a curse. And this is why it was central to the economic renewal practice of jubilee. Relationship to land functioned as the cornerstone to a viable life for families. My own modern experience required a reorientation before I could begin to understand fully the words about land returned to families.

In addition to what land represents for the Batwa, there is the actual challenge of land availability in a country with fewer and fewer land parcels unspoken for and a rapidly increasing population clamoring for property. In our initial community development project with thirty Batwa families, we were able to purchase a large plot with a clean title for them. In the current context that is no longer realistic. We now have to think about communities and collective ownership, and when possible, land granted by the government.

Opportunity for such communities is, again, connected to the land. As we have witnessed, it is found in a future in which the Batwa own agricultural land, attain economic self-sufficiency, realize their full potential for a viable life beyond survival mode. It is found in passing on to future generations the values and resources that enable them to flourish.

As we look at ancient cultures, we see they wrestled with how to hold property. Does it all belong to the king and his royal house? Is it held in common by all? Is the land a commodity for sale? Or a kind of public trust? Israel participated in this conversation—and the land wrestling match.

In the histories recorded in 1 Kings, we see this play out in two brief scenes that involve the prophet Elijah. In the first episode we watch the mighty prophet confront the many prophets of Baal, the Canaanite god active in the region, at Mount Carmel.[1] Canaanites, we might recall from the Hebrew

---

[1] 1 Kings 18:20–40; 21:1–27.

Bible, represented a predatory economy.[2] So this is the god of a predatory economy that Elijah is facing off against in this narrative. Most of us have heard this story preached as a contest between two gods to prove which was the stronger god or the real god. But the narrative turns out to have an additional economic layer of meaning as well. We are invited to discern the two gods—and the economic purview of each. Who would be victorious—the god of the predatory economy or the god of the neighborly economy shaped by a commitment to justice? Which one would light a fire without a match and bring an end to the drought at hand?

In this duel between deities, carried out by their prophetic proxies, YHWH defeated Baal. The god of Elijah, and the neighborly economy of Elijah's god, won the day. Jewish women and men knew that this meant the world must operate differently—more neighborly, less predatory.

To interact with the second scene we move east from Mount Carmel to the Jezreel Valley. King Ahab, likely from the balcony of his palace, spies some land. It is not his royal parcel, but the vineyard just beyond it belonging to his neighbor and subject Naboth. He wants it. So the king goes to Naboth and makes an offer he doubts Naboth can refuse: "Give me your vineyard so I can have it for a vegetable garden, since it is near my house. I am willing to give you a better vineyard in exchange—or give you its value in money."

Naboth refuses the offer. His reason? He could not give his god-given ancestral inheritance away, not to the king and not for any amount of money. This was a jubilary response. Not everything is for sale. Some things remain in a family portfolio—like land. We are told the king walks home sullen and resentful. He really had an amazing garden planned for

---

[2] "'Canaanite' is not an ethnic term. It is rather an ideological term that . . . connotes a predatory economy" (Walter Brueggemann, *Money and Possessions: Interpretation—Resources for the Use of Scripture in the Church* [Westminster John Knox Press, 2016], 35).

that plot. He returns to his royal chamber and pouts, refusing to even eat.

His wife, Jezebel, goes to check in on him. She learns the source of his sadness—and cannot believe that Naboth refused his king. This would not be tolerated in her native Canaan. But equally baffling is her husband accepting the answer and not simply taking what he wanted. She decides to step in and solve the problem the Canaanite way.

Jezebel set a trap for Naboth. She sent a word on royal letterhead to some local leaders, giving them instructions to falsely accuse Naboth in a public setting, and make sure doing so results in a public stoning. These men do as she directed. And all too soon Naboth, the good neighbor, was murdered.

Once word arrives that Naboth was dead, she told Ahab to go and take possession of the vineyard and begin gardening. And so he does just that. If this was a Canaanite city, this would likely be the end of the story. But this is YHWH's land, YHWH's economy, and so YHWH's rules.

The Lord summons Elijah. "Go to meet King Ahab. . . . He is now in the vineyard of Naboth." And so Elijah catches the king in the act of taking possession of land that, according to YHWH, is not his. The prophet delivered a divine pronouncement, a death announcement for both King Ahab and his queen, Jezebel.

It is noteworthy that this scene is peppered with actions that echo the Decalogue, those ten commands Moses carried down from Mount Sinai to guide behavior as the people began to build a new society outside of Egypt. Jezebel plotted to bear false witness against Naboth, and she upped the ante by persuading others to join in the lie. Together, they participated in his murder. Then she and Ahab seized the land he had coveted from the beginning.[3] They broke faith with their

---

[3] Richard Horsley explains that the command against coveting is actually about land seizure, not just wanting what belongs to another but scheming to take it. This is perfectly exemplified in the story of Naboth's

neighbor and disobeyed God. No wonder, in the logic of the biblical text, they were left to the dogs.[4]

What is at stake is land intended to remain in the hands of Naboth and his kin. The land belongs to God, not the king. God has gifted this vineyard to a family in perpetuity; it is their ancestral inheritance. The land is not for sale. And if, in the rough and tumble of the economy, it was ever lost, it would eventually be restored to the family in accordance with jubilee practices. Someone in the family would redeem it. Or the man could buy it back if he came across the funds in the future. Worst case scenario, he would wait until the fiftieth year, when the shofar blew across the land. Then at last the deed would be given back to him and his family.[5]

But King Ahab coveted the land. And after Jezebel's predatory antics, he took possession of the land. He knew better. He knew that land was never his to possess for a garden or any other purpose. As for Jezebel, she acted in accordance with the Canaanite economic practices around land acquisition that did not heed a Mosaic covenant, practice jubilee, or practice neighborly economics. She preyed upon Naboth so the king could seize the land he coveted for a vegetable garden.

Sadly, land seizure continues to happen. Forced migration from one parcel to another also occurs to benefit some and deepen the disadvantage of the vulnerable. Claude and I have seen this happen in real time.

∼

It began with a phone call in 2012. The government pushed the Batwa off the land because they "needed" it for a cemetery.

---

vineyard. See Richard Horsley, *Covenant Economics: A Biblical Vision of Justice for All* (Westminster John Knox, 2009).

[4] King Ahab does repent and is spared the blood death described by Elijah. But his descendants are not spared, nor is Jezebel.

[5] These three options for land return are spelled out in Leviticus 25:25–28.

Our friend Ntazina called to let us know that they were moving from their makeshift village—the one where Claude met them that first day. It was the phone call that would set us on the path of expanding our community development work.

The government pointed the Batwa families to a barren swath of land down the road in the province of Bubanza. And it was there Claude and I drove out to meet them in their new place. There were 660 families who banded together for the move. We arrived to find them constructing small huts out of dried grass. The soil was more like thin, brown dirt. Nothing seemed to grow in the vicinity, making the plot worthless and therefore considered suitable for the Batwa families. This shriveled-up land vividly displayed the government's disdain. The inhospitality of the land was exacerbated by the merciless sun beating down, not a tree in sight for a shady reprieve. There was no housewarming gift we could offer that would make this place feel much like home.

A few days later Ntazina called again. The soldiers who loitered around the edges of their new village made contact, telling the families they had to move to the backside of the hill. They did not like the fact that the Batwa families and their grass huts could be seen from the main road. They needed to start again on the far side and be invisible—all 660 families.

This is what it was like to be Batwa in Burundi. They had to obey; they had no rights or leverage to put up a fight. Ntazina knew Claude would visit again soon, so he called Claude to let him know they were still there, just out of sight from the road.

We rushed out there. Claude refused to accept such ugliness, such disregard for these families. He didn't want them to be forced to start their huts over, to be further from the road, to accept invisibility.

Making his way to the soldiers, Claude offered his first defense for his friends. But this was above the paygrade of the young soldiers. He would have to meet the chief of the zone or some other government functionary. At least for a few days he was able to negotiate a stop to the forced move, buying him time to find a more permanent resolution.

One permanent result that emerged was our partnership with these families. As Claude and I advocated on their behalf, we spoke with our partners in Texas. Their ample generosity meant that we did not need to seek out other donors and support. They were eager to help support this community development project. Claude then met with not only the chief of the zone in Bubanza, but the general in charge of the region and the governor of the province. He told the governor that these families needed the plot in perpetuity—no more moving. He reminded him that they could be permanent residents—and voters in future local elections. Maybe embracing them would be politically strategic, Claude insinuated. It worked—eventually.

The most immediate result of Claude's advocacy was that the families did not have to move to the backside of the hill. And we began active work with them to make this land, such as it was, a home. It was poor quality soil, but at least there was a plan in place to prevent forced migration. Our inaugural initiative was planting trees to provide a break from the hot winds, to offer shade as the trees grew, and to enrich the soil for the future.

Our team began to secure identity cards for each adult in the community. This meant multiple weeks of paperwork and photos. We brought appropriate government officials out to sign all the documents necessary to finalize the identity cards. And as the cards became available, we'd deliver batches of one hundred at a time.

Claude decided to begin by obtaining cards for all the women. So they received their cards first—with much celebration. I remember the final batch of three-hundred cards. Our friends had just arrived in Burundi, René from South Africa, and Idelette and Tina from Canada. These women had been working for many weeks to raise funds for identity cards for the women, $12 each for 660 women added up to nearly

$9,000 raised. And they landed in time to hand out the final batch of light blue ID cards to these Batwa women.

Claude put the ID cards in the hands of Idelette, Tina, and René and let them distribute them. Each card was presented by a woman to a woman, each with a tight embrace and often with tears. The women began dancing and singing, ID cards held high over their heads with joy. "Now I am a full person!" Donetella announced. Another woman said that now the police could not hold her in jail for the crime of walking without proper documentation. She could go to the market with confidence because now she had an identity card, and as a citizen she could not be harassed anymore. It was another jubilary moment, seeing these women finally feel a sense of belonging to their land and having freedom of movement within it. That day we danced till our feet ached with the weight of goodness.

There are days like that, where jubilee is realized. Where it is utterly tangible. Where you know in your body it is real and worth all the effort.

The other marker of belonging that our Batwa friends required was one that affected children: birth certificates. They can be hard to secure. But they are necessary for children to receive medical care at a government-sponsored health clinic. And when Claude saw the small caskets buried week after week as he worked in Bubanza, he knew the community could not wait. The team fast tracked birth certificates for the most fragile children.

A few days before the first large batch of birth certificates was ready, Claude went to the nearby clinic. He told them to be ready, because in three days there would be a long line of mamas with their babies in need of immediate care. For the record, that is exactly how it happened. The mothers walked together with their babies, birth certificates, and identity cards to the small clinic to get medical treatment.

Soon the ID cards came in for all the men, and the celebration was complete. Claude took photocopies of all the identity cards to the governor. "These are your new constituents," he announced, pushing the photocopies across the desk. The governor looked through the pages and realized that each person listed this plot of land as a permanent address. And with all the paperwork properly done and signed by the appropriate people, he could not deny their place in Bubanza. So that day they made it official—this is their land in perpetuity. They would not be moved. Jubilee struck again in the governor's office, thanks in good measure to a shrewd jubilee practitioner.

In the thirteen years since, Bubanza has bloomed. Because the land belonged to them, they could enthusiastically partner with us and our friends at Community of Faith in Houston to develop the community. So we dug wells with solar-powered hydraulic pumps to bring the water taps right into the center of the community. We started an elementary school for their children and hired the best educators we could find. We opened a trade school to make sure young adults were not left out, but learned about agriculture, sewing, construction, mechanics, and soap making. Now they have jobs to support their growing families. We opened a health clinic focused on maternal health and pediatric care, ensuring that mothers and their babies would benefit from a strong start. Of course, in times of trouble like a malaria outbreak and the COVID pandemic, our clinic became a vital resource for the entire province of Bubanza, allowing this community to be a blessing to its neighbors in need.

Driving to visit our friends is different now. From the road we see hills of green, mature trees waving us in. As we enter the community center, there are flowers of all colors. Little homes, not huts, have windows and doors and often small vegetable gardens. Children are laughing and running at recess. Mothers sit in the shade as they wait for their appointment with the doctor for a checkup, more fortified porridge, or a vaccine for their child. People crowd around the water taps, filling their bowls and bottles with clean, filtered water. These families are not merely surviving, they are living better lives.

Jubilee possesses a generative force. Land and lives benefit. One jubilee action activates another. Trees bless the soil, identity cards secure belonging, birth certificates ensure access to basic medical care, and land becomes a permanent home to be developed and cherished. Of course, it also took a jubilee practitioner who cared about this Batwa community. Jubilee requires strategy. The land could not be developed until the families possessed the deed; otherwise, the government could take it again with all the improvements. So identity cards first opened the door to the deed, and then to development.

Jubilee also required someone shrewd, who knew how to maneuver around the political realities on the ground, and knew how to cajole the chief of the zone and the governor to see the Batwa as residents worthy of respect. And jubilee practitioners need to be long-suffering, because it took many years before we could see this community strong and stable, able to stand tall in a good land of its own.

∼

While jubilee is about our communities, it is also about our families. These ways of seeing the needs of our own kin and responding with small yet significant kindnesses echo jubilary goodness. I recall Claude and his relationship with his Aunt Leonie, a woman in need of a little extra goodness. Her entry into his life happened before he was even brought home from the hospital.

Mama Rose had several small children underfoot—and another on the way. Her husband, Andre, knew she would need help when the new baby arrived. He trekked up-country and asked his sister to move in with his growing family and oversee the care of his soon to be born son, Claude.

Leonie raised Claude. She never left the Nikondeha home. She spent her years tending to him, his younger siblings, and eventually, her own daughter. Her reliability, loyalty, and kindness made her a fixture in the day-to-day life of the family. Once all the kids had grown, married and moved out, she kept a small apartment in the family compound. And when Andre and Mama Rose moved out to seek medical care in Canada, she stayed and managed the property. She collected rent from the family that moved into the house and the relatives who rented the other small studios within the family plot. She diligently deposited the money in Andre's bank account, not keeping a penny for herself.

There was no one Claude trusted more than Leonie. When we decided to adopt our son and daughter, he recruited her much as his father did years before. She taught Claude how to bathe the babies and feed them. She became a comforting presence for them in those early months when they transitioned into our Burundian home. She functioned like a third parent. Since I did not speak the local language, I appreciated her taking the kids to doctor appointments. She helped with meals and cleaning, ever available to help our family.

When our kids entered high school, she moved with us to a new home. She helped care for Mama Rose, who was falling into the shadows of dementia. She was still there for my kids when they came home each day. She still made some of their favorite meals.

But Leonie now had a grown daughter and grandchildren. And when she wasn't with us, she was with them, offering the same care. She took what little she had from her salary (she worked at a local organization equipping Sunday School teachers) and a stipend from us to support them. She never married, never had property or a home to pass on to her daughter. And she worried about that, because her daughter had a husband who could not provide those things for her, either.

After all she had given to Claude, all she had given to our children, we knew we wanted to be more than generous with her. We wanted to be a channel of jubilee goodness to her. Claude told me that the best and most lasting gift we could give her would be a home of her own, a plot with her name on the deed. This would not only be a home for her now, but an inheritance she could pass on to her daughter, and then could be given to her grandchildren.

With a plan, we quietly began saving until we had what was needed.

Just last year Claude told Leonie we wanted to purchase a plot for her to ensure that she had a home of her own. He told her to find something suitable, something that met her standard for a family home. And when she did, Claude purchased it in her name. She now has her own home. She has an inheritance for her daughter and grandchildren. She knows they will always have a home, a place that is theirs. For her, it is jubilee.

~

I think it is beautiful, how sometimes jubilee comes quietly in small ways laden with love, like Leonie's house. Other times jubilee is a heavy lift requiring group effort, strategy, and some clever moves affecting wider communities. It brings to mind something Jesus said about how to move in a fraught landscape, advice to be as "wise as serpents and innocent as doves."[6] Watching Claude over the years, I can clearly see this applies to jubilee practitioners too. The jubilary way is seldom straightforward, especially as we translate these ancient practices to complex, modern economies.

Securing land, honoring home, and making inheritance possible are all elements of jubilee we can practice, even if the mechanisms are different now. And then there is this: jubilee practitioners advocate for *home*. They intuitively know that it is not just property. It is not about unattached families. A cornerstone of the jubilee mission is securing a home for every family.

~

Chapter 25 of the Book of Leviticus announces the grand plan of jubilee, what happens when the shofar sounds off across the land in the fiftieth year. "You shall return . . . to your

---

[6] Matthew 10:16.

property," is the first imperative.[7] Everyone gets to go home. Jubilee begins with your literal place in the world. And *home* is the right word, as it encompasses place and family, both of which are spelled out in the Mosaic law.

Continuing with the jubilee decree, Moses posits that these rules function to ensure that "you may live on the land securely." "The land shall not be sold in perpetuity," for it belongs to God. This reality makes everyone on the land a tenant. It is the responsibility of the tenant "to provide for the redemption of the land."[8]

Again, we are cast in the role of steward for the capital that belongs to God alone. The text may use terms like debtor and creditor when it comes to land management, but both are ultimately known to God as tenants.

The law goes into detail about how land ought to be managed. If anyone falls into debt and sells ancestral land to service the debt, there are three ways provided to redeem it. First, if his financial situation changes, he can purchase the land back at any time. Second, A relative can purchase the land from the creditor and restore it to the family. If neither of those mechanisms materialize, then the jubilee year will come and his deed will be returned.[9] Jubilee is the safety net. Jubilee ensures return to land and family. Jubilee ensures that you get to go home.

~

I often think of those in our modern world who are barred from home. Palestinian families were refused the right of return after the Nakba, and to this very day. They carry keys to homes they can no longer enter. On my own continent there are the First Nations peoples who live on reservations or other lands,

---

[7] Leviticus 25:10, 13.
[8] Leviticus 25:18, 23, 24.
[9] Leviticus 25:25–28.

but not where their roots are intertwined with the soil. All the broken treaties with the US government forced migration, making most tribal peoples forever displaced. Then there are the Dreamers, the children of immigrants born in the United States who know no other home. Yet they live a precarious existence, dependent on the results of each election to know if their status will be protected or not. Will they be sent to a foreign land, away from the only home they've ever known? And what of those pushed out of homes with eviction notices or who fall prey to foreclosure on their family home? In our world, in its economies and conflicts, *home* can be quite elusive.

Yet the call and invitation of Jubilee is about *being home* in God's world, living a viable life with your family in a secure place. As jubilee practitioners we can become advocates for home—and for returning home. We can honor the ache of reunion between people and their ancestral lands. We can see the land as created for goodness, and ourselves as irrevocably connected to it. Jubilee gives tangible expression to that sacred relationship between humanity and land. We see it as holy.

Part Three

The Possibilities of Jubilee

7

Loss and Lament

Before the fire, before the porridge factory, before gathering the families in Matara . . . we felt the sting possible in jubilary work.

Early on we joined with four Batwa friends, forming a working committee. Our initial endeavor, at their request, centered on secondary education. Together we created a program for a student house in which about twenty students could reside as they attended high school in the capital city. Their housing would include reliable utilities like water and electricity, often not available in their villages up-country. They would receive funding for tuition and uniforms and school supplies. The house would be a safe place for the students, free from discrimination and with cultural empowerment provided by local Batwa leaders. Together we envisioned a better situation for the students to learn, where there was light to study into the night, and rain would not drench their clothes and text books. Where there would be ample food to fuel their brains for the academic work. Our highest hope was that among the students who graduated would be future leaders for Burundi.

We spent time with the Batwa committee shaping and running the program. We spent even more time at the student house for training sessions, report-card reviews, and celebrations. We watched some graduate and new students take their places. There was reason to hope that this was working.

But at some point Claude discerned an emerging dynamic he found problematic. Students were opting out of visits home during holiday breaks, some even refusing to return to their villages for the summer months. They preferred the student house with all the utilities, reliable meals, and other niceties their village homes lacked. Understandable. But what worried Claude was the growing disconnection from their communities, their families, and fathers. In Burundian culture the patriarch of the family is honored, and his company and counsel are sought out by his children. But when the students started seeking Claude's counsel for matters youth would traditionally share with fathers, he knew we'd made a structural mistake. He was gutted, realizing a distance was growing between the students and their villages and between the students and their fathers and families.

We began to reconsider our model.

As we wrestled with a flawed model, a heavier blow landed. One committee member, believing there was more money designated for student housing than we were sharing, contacted our funders behind our backs. Pascal (not his real name) accused us of pocketing extra funds for ourselves. In Burundi, one of the by-products of colonization is the ever-present suspicion that someone is making money off you—especially if you are the middle man between the community and an institution (like a nonprofit organization or a church). And Pascal had lived his entire life in the clutches of colonization—scammed, used, betrayed. Participation in our committee was his first real chance at respect and influence. He was on the lookout for anything, anyone, who might threaten his place.

All the time we invested in cultivating friendships with these leaders and sharing openly and honestly still didn't protect us from this kind of rampant distrust. We had nothing to hide, and so when we learned of the situation, we allowed the line of inquiry to play out, knowing our innocence and financial fidelity to the funds would clear the question. But what suffered a significant blow was the trust between us and our four friends on the working committee, as the other three instinctively rallied around Pascal, connected and loyal to their shared family ties.

At home, after we learned of the situation, we held hands and sat at the edge of our bed wondering what we could have done differently. We cried as we considered the failed model we could—and did—reimagine. As we felt a rift in our relationships.

We knew much of long-term development work involves trial and error and an openness to adjustments along the way. So we made necessary changes, and after the initial set of students all graduated, we decided to discontinue the program.

To preserve community connection while supporting students, we moved to a community-based education model. This was the easier part of the painful process as we moved toward a remedy.

The betrayal. That stung. How could our friends think we would steal from them? After all the meals together in our home, all the cups of coffee shared at Aroma Coffee Shop, after all the visits to their villages? After protecting land, so they could call it their own? After supporting their children for a bright future? Of course, how could they think differently, when so many others over the years had betrayed them. Their experience of a community at the hands of a colonial environment told them nothing—no one—would treat them differently. They would not let themselves be used by us, so one of them got out ahead and, in making accusations against us, then tried to benefit from the arrangement.

In retrospect, we understand better. We acknowledge the layers of power structures, generations of navigating colonial architecture, deep effects of trauma, and a community's desire for self-preservation. Those forces conspired together and pummeled us. It may not have been personal to our four friends, but the betrayal felt acutely personal to us.

For a long while we wrestled in a dark place, mourning the true state of the relationship Pascal's actions revealed. Some relationships were, in fact, transactional. Through all this, what came to the fore was my own questioning of our purpose, our work. In those tumultuous days it was the first time I asked Claude if all this was worth our love and labor. And it was also the first time I realized a commitment to jubilee work could set us up for a bruising.

Even as we worked to repair the friendships, Pascal was forever lost to us. The scar, the grief, remains to this day.

While we have worked for over fifteen years as jubilee practitioners with much success, situations like the student house and the betrayals revealed to us and to others that not all projects we began on behalf of communities have endured. *Durability* is something I've lost sleep over, shed tears over. Why do some—sometimes more than some—of our jubilary efforts seem to evaporate? Why isn't there a ripple effect that alters the local landscape in Bujumbura? Why can't we witness a lasting transformation producing a better economy for Burundians?

We've witnessed communities fall back into economic hardship. We've seen people we supported with capital and training experience financial viability for a handful of years, only to succumb to the precarity of the fiscal landscape. Some of the enterprises built on jubilee principles needed to be retired.

If so many outcomes are ephemeral, we began to ask if we were doing it right. Is jubilee up to the task? Can it transform modern economies for the sake of those too often exploited by them?

The truth is that Burundi's economy is unraveling despite our jubilary tenure there. Claude used to always tell me, back in the early days of our marriage, that we could make a big impact in a small country like Burundi. On the lips of most that might be a cliché, but Claude is a social entrepreneur unlike most. I believed him—and believed that with sustained jubilee efforts we could see tangible transformation.

But the waters of Lake Tanganyika continue to rise due to climate change. And low-lying communities continue to be flooded, as well as the Burundi port, the United Nations compound, World Relief office complex, a mosque, and critical roads. The country has been without a steady supply of fuel, both petrol and diesel, for over a year, resulting in a standstill in transportation—no minibuses or taxis on the road—making it harder for people to get to work.

The electrical grid, built in the colonial era for a smaller population, is showing signs of its age. Routinely the lights and power now go out in neighborhoods, the industrial sector, and even the downtown economic center of the city. All those generators that have been a backup strategy for power? They sit empty, with no fuel to keep them running.

A perfect storm is battering the already fragile economy. And in this current climate, we are trying to keep a bank, a radio station, a porridge factory, and other development projects afloat. It's been rough.

Many of the people we partner with fall behind, drop out despite our best jubilee efforts. "How are you not discouraged?" I asked Claude recently.

Looking at me, he said: "I know that our partnership with a businesswoman allowed her to experience economic stability for a season. For several years she had a good business that enabled her to put her girls through school and have food on the table each night." He talked about another person who was able to build a home for his family while his business operated at a profit. Some earn a better wage for just long enough to cover medical expenses at a critical time or take a trip to visit family. Even these short-term gains matter, he said.

Perhaps his own early years growing up in a precarious economy enables him to see even temporal viability as good reason for our efforts. He does not expect a steady economic landscape, even as he yearns for one with all its benefits.

In this environment I watch as he considers any stretch of fiscal prosperity an opportunity for celebration. And he knows, too, there are too many who cannot stitch together even a single season of a viable life, despite our attempts to help. Malnourishment, colonial pedagogies, and other factors play a part in the truncated capacity.[1]

But the frustration is real for Claude, too. And it is a good grace that we are rarely in the depths of discouragement at the same time. Usually one of us buoys the other through the storms of doubt, disappointment, and sometimes even the sinkhole of disillusionment.

But I sit back and think about Shebani, who suffered a late-onset disease and lost the use of his legs. His family did not know how to manage a son with a disability in their rural community with uneven roads, no access to wheelchairs, or any other accommodations. So Shebani decided to make his way to the city of Bujumbura. He started selling phone credit at a centrally located petrol station. He worked his way up, eventually getting a wheelchair and then enough success to employ others. Claude invited him to membership in Kazoza Bank in our first year, which provided him with the capital to grow his business and the training to manage that growth.

Year by year Shebani has grown his enterprise from the corner of the petrol station, where he is now a well-known fixture. He has a good savings account, has purchased a small plot, built a modest home, and recently married. He has found his way forward.

Amid the hard news is the better news that now, even if Kazoza Bank no longer existed, he would still thrive. His success is sustainable. So every time we drive by the station and wave to Shebani, my heart is full, knowing jubilee practices moved him away from the perils of poverty, prevented him from falling into debt, and allowed him to find his path toward

---

[1] For more on colonial pedagogies, see the work of Paulo Freire, especially his seminal book *Pedagogy of the Oppressed* (Seabury Press, 1970).

prosperity. "All this would be worth it," Claude once said, "if we only helped Shebani."

∽

Jubilary practitioners are not alone in the struggle. The prophet Isaiah writes about the failed urban economy of Jerusalem in his time. It failed due to greed, corruption, and all manner of injustices. This economic maleficence and disregard for the poor, the foreigners, the eunuchs, and others, the prophet said, weakened the nation, making it vulnerable to defeat by a foreign power. Within the logic of the biblical text God allowed this destruction to happen to Jerusalem, the holy city and epicenter of public life. This failure taught Israel a necessary lesson about how the nation ought to function. God's chosen people met with the utter destruction of Jerusalem and forced exile of the elites to Babylon. What a devastating loss. What a perfect storm of losses.

For Isaiah, *loss* is where his story of Jerusalem begins. And loss is where we, too, began to understand the story of Burundi's situation.[2] What does it look like to begin with loss? It means engaging with the understanding that loss matters. That grieving matters.

Over the years, acknowledging loss and beginning there have formed the fundamental first act in our community development process. We ask what dynamics on the ground contribute to the economic duress Burundians experience, what are the contours of loss. For our Batwa friends we named the reality they described and we witnessed—landlessness, lack of standing, lack of human rights protections, tribal discrimination, lack of basic education and healthcare. This wretched economic

---

[2] A sermon by Walter Brueggemann given at Mars Hill Church in Grand Rapids, Michigan, in July 2008, presented a powerful articulation of this arc in Isaiah and Lamentationsm which informs much of my writing and our work informed by loss, lament, hope, and hard work. Brueggemann has given me his permission to use his framework in my writing.

condition that kept the Batwa families on the bloodied edge of survival is where we began.

They revealed the depth of their collective pain. We listened; we cried; we shared tears; we clasped hands; we embraced as they gave testimony of lament. Some nights we sat in stunned silence after our Batwa friends left our home, unable to find words to hold the weight of our sadness.

After a devastating flood, when the Red Cross quickly erected a camp, Claude joined the tent where the women had only tears in the wake of losing homes—and even children—in the waters. He added his tears to theirs. In the thick of the darkness, he joined others in lamenting the losses.

In the arc of our development work, the second act is lament. Sometimes it collapses into the first act, with loss and lament grasping hands, but it is always present somewhere in our work. The Book of Lamentations insists to Isaiah that grief must have its say.[3] Yes, the Babylonians laid waste to Jerusalem and took many into captivity. And those who remained in the ruins cried out in anguish. Loss calls out; lament responds.

Fellow jubilee practitioners, we speak to you. The prophets speak to you. Often the story of jubilee change begins here. Obey the sadness, make room in your work for lament. Do not rush too quickly to solutions.

Across the years it has been naming loss and entering lament that have grounded our community development work. What we have learned, we have shared with other practitioners, encouraging them to do the same. Take time to see the losses of your community. Find the language for what you see, as though you were naming the territory of loss and lament on an unmarked map. Understand that the landscape of loss is

---

[3] Walter Brueggemann notes the location of Lamentations between 1 Isaiah and 2 Isaiah—"a response to the long period of dislocation, during which the exiles voiced their grief and dismay"—in his commentary on Isaiah. See Walter Brueggemann, *Isaiah 40–66* (Westminster John Knox Press, 1998), 15–16. In a sermon given to Mars Hill Church in July 2008 he expounds on the connection, calling Lamentations the grief work of the Old Testament.

Loss and Lament

the entry point to connecting with any community you seek to partner with for the sake of development.

We began to approach the economics of jubilee in Burundi by listening to loss and surveying the dynamics that impinged on the economy. We asked what local exigencies prevented women and men from growing their business, even when many exhibited an intuitive business sense. Through analysis and grief we began to name the gap between microlending and commercial loan sizes, we named the need to create new banking instruments and policies to partner with these business people. And as we saw, even in the sphere of banking we could not avoid lament. The marketplace fire brought loss to our gate, and so too, the need to lament.

When Claude and I teach seminars on our theology of development, it's not uncommon for pastors and leaders to ask me to dial down (or completely omit) talk of lament. They think people need inspiration and instruction, not conversations around sadness. But know this: when it comes to educating about lament, I am all gas and no brakes. Why? Because I've learned that community leaders light up when I talk about lament in connection with their work. When community leaders learn that emotions belong in the arc of their work, they heaved a sigh of recognition and relief. And that achingly deep empathy they feel for those families they labor alongside? When they also witness it in the ancient biblical text as an integral part of community care, they get it. They are not scandalized by sadness. They are relieved that it has a name and a place in healthy practice. They know it as the beginning. They know that mourning with those who mourn matters. Pastors and leaders may be out of touch with lament, but on-the-ground practitioners have no such luxury.

For how can we witness destruction and not feel the sorrow of loss? Our humanity demands we share the sadness of our neighbors. It is a beginning. Weeping together is the predicate to rejoicing together in jubilary celebrations. That is why our economic work follows the trajectory set by Isaiah and Lamentations, because embracing loss and lament is the necessary movement in the work of community transformation.

Yes, atrocities keep coming, loss upon loss. But what we now know is that landing in the space of lament is not permanent and often can be the catalyst for what comes next. We don't shrink from our sadness and the pain of the communities we partner with. We know lament is the seedbed of hope.

We labor toward collective transformation. This includes advocating for human rights, better housing, and healthcare; and working for improved education access, improved agriculture, and also a better economy. All these elements work together when we talk about community viability and societal health. We understand the economy is part of the community development purview. Economics are integral to a full-bodied community transformation.

We recognize the economy is plagued with loss suffered by many. In our American context of late-stage capitalism, where corporate interests reign supreme, we see an economy wired for the rich to get richer and the poor to fall further into poverty. Like Jerusalem of old that Isaiah spoke of, it is an exploitative economy that does violence to many of our neighbors. The same was true in the days of the pharaonic economy. No wonder so many cry out for relief.

Such economic stress experienced by the masses creates unrest. The human pattern across centuries reveals how discontent foments the conditions for change. But first we might witness the unleashing of instability and fear into society, which all too often invites an authoritarian response. If we look to Germany in the 1920s, for example, we see that its period of hyperinflation paved the way for Hitler and the Nazi regime: a strong man voted into power to ease economic anxieties, which eventually contributed to the rise of the Third Reich and the Final Solution. That economies play a fundamental role in social change should be no surprise, moving us as they do toward our better angels or darker demons. But this is a lesson any aspiring jubilee practitioner should heed.

Functioning economies matter to societal stability and health. Therefore, the cornerstone to community care is tending to the economy. And no conversation about transforming societies can be complete without attention to the economies that underpin them. The economy must serve families, not oligarchs, in ways that allow families and workers to participate in and fund a viable life within the community. Isaiah tells us, within the biblical world, that it was a weakened economy that contributed to the demise of Jerusalem.[4]

Perhaps American anxieties about inflation in a post-pandemic landscape took the nation to the cliff's edge. Similar dynamics in the wake of the pandemic tipped elections across the world toward authoritarianism. Societies yearning for pluralism, where people of all different beliefs and practices, origins and orientations can live together as good neighbors, are under threat. When we work for deep transformation, we ignore economies to the detriment of our communities.

Minding the economy invites conversations about loss and lament, about realities on the ground and repair required, and calls for a fair amount of collaborative imagination. Such conversations might demand that we parlay our fears into curiosity about the machinations of the economies we participate in. We might start noticing the gaps and who is falling prey to them. Maybe we start observing the dynamics that contribute to those pitfalls. And then we reach for tools of a jubilary nature to address the economic duress that besets far too many and makes them susceptible to authoritarian tendencies triggered by community fears.

Once we truly see the economic landscape, we can reach for tools honed by jubilee. We can cancel debt. We can return land or renegotiate how it is held and managed. We can enact better labor practices and fairer pay. As jubilee practitioners, we can be guardrails preventing neighbors from falling into

---

[4] Isaiah 1:10–23; 3:14ff.; 5:8.

poverty. We can make sure that on our watch poverty is never a life sentence.

∼

After years as a theologian and liberationist wrestling with the jubilary canon, I arrived at the realization that the collection of jubilee practices form a social safety net. And that healthy communities demand a safety net. There must be protection from poverty, from the regular risks of the economy, for our neighbors. Jubilee sees with wide-eyed clarity the precarity of the economy and responds with the formation of policies to safeguard families from catastrophic loss. Contemporary efforts to create the necessary infrastructure to prevent irretractable indebtedness, job loss, home forfeiture, and all manner of economic duress have the fingerprints of jubilee. When we work against the calcification of the economy, laboring to keep it open for others to enter or reenter, we do good work that aligns with the jubilary efforts of our ancestors.

Jubilee has been implemented many times across human history, from Sumer to Israel to Burundi. It has worked to protect and rescue the most vulnerable of society. No, it has not worked perfectly in all times and places. Throughout history its application has been uneven. But when jubilee is embraced by practitioners, short-term and sometimes even long-term transformation *is* possible.

Our remit is not only to practice jubilee, but to investigate both its potential and limitations. We wrestle with modern applications of these practices, and we remain curious about the contemporary efficacy of jubilee endeavors.

Claude and I—pragmatist within a context and theologian reaching for the economic landscape of the new city—work as a team. He takes what wins we can get in the here and now and builds on them. I look for a vision of what can be. Together we have aimed to embody the jubilee imperative.

∼

Beyond the scars of that student-house project stand two women, Charlotte and Imelda. We met them both when they were students in the initial project. Each completed high school. Each one continued her education and found a career serving the Batwa community.

When in 2023 the Burundian government announced the creation of a Truth and Reconciliation Commission (similar to South Africa's years ago), it said this commission would address the crimes and resulting trauma of the civil-war years. It was a huge move the government made toward accountability and healing. And amid this news of change, Charlotte resurfaced, selected to be on this historic committee.

After high school she went on to become a registered nurse and serve in a local hospital. She was known as a force for good among her colleagues, her patients, and her community. It was her name that rose to the top of the list as a credible and compassionate advocate to represent her people on the Truth and Reconciliation Commission. In the thirteen years since she graduated from our student program, she has been making a national impact in the story of Burundian healing.

Imelda, also a student at the house, graduated as well, continuing her education and gaining a degree in human rights advocacy, with a passion to defend the vulnerable, especially those communities that historically experienced discrimination.

In 2021 Imelda was invited by the president of Burundi to join his cabinet to represent marginalized groups across the country as the nation's advocate for human rights for all Burundian citizens who experienced discrimination. She is the first Batwa to serve in the presidential cabinet, as well as the highest ranking Batwa in the government to date. Now when we see her, we address her as Honorable Imelda, or Honorable for short.

All these years later, after heartbreak and loss and lament, green sprouts push through the dark loam into the daylight. These women embody our highest hopes for the student house:

to support the future leaders of Burundi. As Claude says, it was all worth it for Charlotte and Honorable, two young leaders for the country. May all our tears water the soil in which they flourish and grow sprouts of hope.

8

Hope and Hard Work

The first time Claude mentioned the idea of starting a bank, I resisted. What did we know about banking? Would we fall prey to the dreaded "mission shift" that befell so many others if we agreed to this prospect? Would the time and energy invested in this new project rob from our current work among our Batwa friends, their communities, and efforts toward their viability? All of it felt like a risk.

Slowly I learned the wisdom of entering the economic fray. Slowly I began to see jubilee economics at play. And with it, economics as foundational to community development.

In the early days of our partnership with the thirty Batwa families in Matara and the student house project, Claude's work drew some quiet attention from development leaders who heard about his model. Curiosity lured Sam, the country director for an international NGO, to Matara to find out more about the work.[1] He pulled Claude aside one day. He had questions about our model. He wanted to hear how we accomplished in just one year what his organization targeted as a ten-year goal. That was when he asked Claude for a favor. Would Claude consult on one of their flailing projects?

That's how the bank conversation started. Sam said the initiative at hand was a microfinance program. In the wake

---

[1] His name has been changed to protect him and the organization that employed him.

of the success of Grameen Bank in Bangladesh, and especially after founder Muhammad Yunus won the Nobel Peace Prize for his work in 2006, many development organizations rushed to launch their own version of microlending projects.[2] The challenge they didn't foresee was the vast difference between the NGO mindset and that of a financial institution or a bank, which was structured to handle money and manage a loan portfolio.

Claude dove into two months of consulting work, finally giving his definitive analysis to Sam. The reason his team ran its program into the ground, he said, was that it treated the program like just another development project under the organization's wide umbrella. But this, Claude said, was a *loan* program. It required financial structures, protocols, accountants.

Claude concluded that as the project was currently constructed, the program would only last another couple of months before the donor funds were dry and only a minuscule return on their anticipated investment trickled in. As Claude assessed the project, he identified another part of the equation that was contributing to the issues: no one among the project's client base had devised a plan to repay the loans. Without detailing the nature of the loan to clients, the organization's reputation for handouts may have confused many, who assumed the loans were a type of gift rather than loans to be repaid.

The hard truth the project faced was little-to-no repayment. And the hard truth the eight hundred Burundian clients were soon to face was a deadline on loan repayment, when the means for repayment were nowhere in sight. And if the project failed and the doors closed, many more who hoped for loans would have no opportunities available.

Then Sam asked Claude the unexpected. Would Claude be willing to assume leadership for the program—manage the program staff, the loan portfolio, and the microlending

---

[2] Muhammad Yunus, *Banker to the Poor* (Aurum Press, 1998). His work has also been heralded in the *New York Times* and by David Bornstein and Jeffery Sachs, among others.

certification from the Central Bank? Claude, he said, would be able to use his innovative mind to rework the program and salvage it. He used win/win language. With Claude leading the project, Sam could tell donors the program was now run by a local to extend its efficacy into the future, allowing the NGO to focus on its core strengths.

That was when Claude and I talked. And when I panicked. While Sam's NGO could now focus on its core strengths and programs, what would this mean for Claude, for me, for our own work? We wrangled through each element: taking over a failing microlending operation, financial responsibility, viability, community benefits, and jubilee (which I was understanding in very nascent form at the time).

Claude felt like this was an invitation to enter into the trenches of transformation work, as by this point in time the enterprise in Matara with thirty families had a natural ceiling. We could only purchase so much land. And while the work benefited those specific families, Claude ached to reach more people with tangible hope for better futures. Through Sam, Claude saw the possibility of serving 97 percent of the Burundian population. These were the unbanked, who needed good tools to save, grow, and manage the little they earned. Entering the economic landscape, he said, could become the way to scale up his transformation portfolio as a jubilee practitioner.

What we didn't even envision then, was that it would also be a generative platform for future work we had yet to even dream of: a radio station for economic education, a porridge factory to fight malnourishment, and environmental work with the United Nations. All this would result from the economic cornerstone of our work. And it started with an attempt to redeem a failing project.

In those days of not knowing, my thin agreement ultimately came not because of the merits of the project, but because I trusted Claude's intuitive sense that this was the next right move in our work to collaborate with and support struggling communities.

Returning to Sam, Claude brought his vision. He made a counter offer. What Sam's NGO started, he said, wasn't salvageable in its current state. Claude proposed a complete spin off.

His research showed—and the current program already revealed—the limits of microlending, which restricted the amount of money going from donors to clients to negligible amounts. For a program to work, he had to be able to take deposits, bringing money in to make the effort sustainable. This would also open the door to right-sized loans for business people ready to grow.

Also, Claude said, he needed an entity entirely separate from the NGO, severing the initiative from any hint of the charity mentality. What he began to envision was a *bank* capable of serving those at the bottom of the economic pyramid, one offering basic banking services to hardworking people like his father. He also wanted to offer financial tools for small business owners so they could grow and possibly employ more people.[3] This plan was revolutionary. This was the seed cracking open, as the tender green of Kazoza Bank slowly unfurled.

While Claude and his team launched the bank, I plunged into the jubilee canon. What I saw revealed there, now that I had eyes to see, was the connection between strong economies and strong families. The biblical purview included economic health as fundamental for families, and entire communities, to thrive. When economies were well structured, people had a chance to do more than just survive. They could afford to hold on to ancestral land and maintain it. They could manage their harvest with ample food for their family and the marketplace. There would even be enough to allow widows to collect the leftovers in the fields, keeping the safety net intact. When the economy held, families could stay together. Well-calibrated economies could better safeguard societies from

---

[3] This is the hybrid banking model mentioned in Chapter 4.

foreign invasions, avoiding the violence of war and trauma in its wake. Strong economies mattered.

The way the prophets drew a line between economies and families made sense to me. Your crops, wheat and figs and pomegranates, need a market. The products you produce like wine and olive oil need buyers. A family needs other families to have the capacity to trade livestock or have the shekels for doves to sacrifice at the temple. This is how each family tends to its primary vocation—survival. And these families, all stitched together, form the communities that weathered empires together.

When the economic inputs align—which must include access to labor and materials, good trade policies, a tax burden not too onerous, and a ruler able to steer clear of regional wars—families stand a chance at living well. Fair scales, curbed corruption, and roads free from banditry contribute to a more workable economy. No wonder they are mentioned throughout the biblical stories. Reading now, it seemed I was finding texts on fair practices in economics throughout scripture. I finally understood that because the God of Israel was for families and neighbors, God was for good economies.

The prophet Isaiah showcased how pivotal the economy was when it came to national stability. According to the logic of the prophet, Israel fell to Babylon due to a failed urban economy that was more predatory than neighborly—or just. Now taken away in chains, the elites became the cheap labor that fueled Babylon's economic boom. Those who remained in the ruins of Jerusalem struggled in a land bereft of all economic infrastructure. The dismal economy made survival harder.

The children lost and families separated, the inability to find food, inadequate housing due to destroyed homes were all due to a war and captivity that the prophet clearly linked to a feeble economy—Israel's injustice-riddled economy—that had invited the invasion.

Across the centuries rapacious economies have resulted in significant loss and lament from the fall of Jerusalem until now. And from the start, the biblical tradition wrestled with such realities, economic inputs and outputs, with clear eyes as the prophets offered constant commentary on the relationship between creditors and debtors, denouncing creditors with strong critiques.[4] Thus, what continued throughout the Hebrew Bible from its laws to its prophets' voicings was continual conversation about debt management and tools for economic renewal. Because these are foundational to the prospect of a stable family and community life. Otherwise, there wasn't just lack, but possibly family separations, migration, and all manner of losses due to violence. A steady economy also meant a greater likelihood for a stable society for every neighbor, every neighborhood.

The work of Isaiah and Lamentations, particularly, provided the infrastructure for our theology of community development: loss and lament followed by hope and much hard work. Jubilee, a policy preference of the prophet, was woven right into the fabric of this vision of transforming the city into something better for everyone. It took Isaiah's words and seeing Claude's vision meet the needs of our community to make clear to me that just economics are the cornerstone to sound development practice. Economics first; development next.

It was with Jubilee that I now moved in growing confidence, into the economic fray, even as I watched Claude's strategy and vision for a nontraditional bank take form. Meting out jubilee in such a concrete way day by day revealed how critical good economics were to families trying to move beyond mere survival. I met with women who shared their good ideas for startup shops filling in gaps in the community, combined with determination. All they needed was a banker willing to

---

[4] Michael Hudson notes that "the Jewish Bible emphasizes the struggle between debtors and creditors as one of its central themes," and that the prophets regularly denounced creditors. Michael Hudson, . . . *And Forgive Us Our Debts: Lending, Foreclosure and Redemption from Bronze Age Finance to the Jubilee Year* (Islet-Verlag, 2018), 181.

partner with them. I saw men with good small businesses other banks ignored finally getting a right-sized loan and support. Businesses sprouted; banking clients boasted signs of new growth. I could not deny the goodness, the signature of jubilee, these women, men, and communities were experiencing due to Kazoza Bank.

So definitive to our work was Kazoza Bank—and later job creation initiatives that have grown out of that vision—that now when people see Claude, they call out "Kazoza!" instead of his given name. He's the man known for the bank and the good future it promises.

∼

Before he was called Kazoza, Claude could have been mistaken for *kwizera* ("hope"). When Claude started working with the Batwa families in Bubanza, recall how he facilitated the process of securing identity cards for all the women and men. And remember that every week he noticed small processions on the far side of the hill—and those tiny coffins. He noticed the sadness winding through the community. He mourned alongside the bereaved parents and that moved him through lament and, eventually, toward hope.[5]

Hope, as Isaiah articulates it, connects to newness. Hope is not a featherweight wish for something better. Rather, hope is more like striking a match providing the spark of a fresh idea that addresses a conundrum too often rooted in one injustice or another. The strike and the spark are hope. And they are the genesis of perennial labor toward justice.

After loss and lament, the third act in our development arc is this striking hope.

The idea to fast track the birth certificates for the sickest children emerged as he walked in one of those funeral

---

[5] The process of obtaining birth certificates to qualify for healthcare is presented in Chapter 6.

processions. The hope-filled idea emerged amid lament. Yes, securing birth certificates added to the workload for the team. But they found the requisite energy—another hallmark of hope. The energy for newness.

Somewhere deep in the well of lament, hope stirs and generates energy for a fresh response to an old problem. Frail children dying too soon seemed a fixture in a place like Burundi, doubly so among the beleaguered Batwa communities with slim resources. If we could get these Batwa babies into the healthcare system, such as it was, as soon as possible, Claude thought, we might prevent more processions. We wanted more birthday candles, not tiny coffins. And so the team prioritized the birth certificates for the most vulnerable.

Then on the horizon of our work came even more new ideas and fresh energy to tackle unemployment, malnourishment, discrimination, even landlessness and deforestation. Hope fueled each enterprise. After the new banking model, hope ignited additional ideas like a primary school, a trade school, and a health clinic with an entire birthing wing all set in the Bubanza community. And it was at this very primary school where the seeds for the porridge factory grew as we tested our initial feeding program with these children. In our community development efforts in Bubanza over the years, hope did a lot of heavy lifting.

For Claude, hope had to be muscular—and make a material difference *today*. Due to his own experience with extreme poverty, he could not tolerate the flimsy and future-oriented hope pedaled by too many missionaries and local pastors. And he came to this intolerance early.

Claude recalls a conversation that transpired amid another "crusade season" in Burundi's hot summer months. He was fourteen, and as the son of a pastor he attended all such revival meetings. While he really wanted to be at the beach with friends, if the visiting evangelists were right about the imminent return of Jesus, he knew he could not play hooky.

But he started to wonder about the annual crusades and the all-too-familiar drumbeat about Jesus returning soon. So he sought out the wisest and most objective man he knew—Gahungu, affectionately known as Mutama, the title for respected elderly men. Mutama was the guard of the church property. He was there every day to open and close the gate, monitoring the activity on site. And while he sat at his post, he entertained Claude's serious question.

"Is Jesus really coming back soon, Mutama? They say it all the time, but is it true?" Mutama told him that the missionaries and pastors said the same thing when he was a little boy living up-country. "I did not want to miss his return, so I got this job guarding the church. Surely this would be the first stop when Jesus comes back! And I've been here ever since. . . . But now I don't believe Jesus is coming anytime soon. I am here for the job to feed my family."

Mutama confirmed what Claude sensed—while there was talk of heavenly hope on the horizon, no one was coming to save his family from poverty, and no one to rescue his neighbors either. As they talked, Claude understood we are trapped in this condition until we extricate ourselves. Hoping for Jesus to return year after year while languishing without a good job, without the ability to go to the doctor, or without a way to feed your children was not a hope Mutama was willing to hold on to anymore. It was in this moment that Claude's notion of a hard-borne hope in its most embryonic form emerged: hope has to be about relief for us *today*.

This is when Claude determined to get out of poverty through education. He began selling fantas (bottled carbonated drinks) to the lorrie drivers lined up outside the coffee-washing station on the edge of his neighborhood to make money for his school fees. He enrolled in the high school with the best record of high national scores, even though it was a Muslim school believed to be founded and funded by Muammar Qaddafi. His national test scores won him a scholarship to university in France. This was how he worked to exit poverty, allowing the sting of poverty and realization that no rescue was under way to activate his own efforts. Many years later he would use that same energy to help others in his community do the same.

Claude connects the ideas from that catalytic conversation at the church gate with Mutama to the day we read Luke's jubilee passage together decades later. Jesus said jubilee, good news, would come *today*. And for Claude it all clicked in place. He said he did not believe in what he called an "evacuation theology" about meeting Jesus in the sky and escaping to heaven. That was not his hope. Instead, it was a hope rooted in the soil of his beloved Burundi, a theology of transformation that would bring tangible hope to the streets where he and his neighbors lived now. In this way he embodies what Miguel De La Torre speaks of in *Embracing Hopelessness*. It is not about a future salvation, but a present liberation that involves an honest wrestling with the hopelessness of the oppressed. That hopelessness can become a holy grist for a true, muscular hope that works for freedom.[6] Claude's own reckoning with his impoverished conditions activated him to push against poverty and not accept it as normative for Burundi. Hope is, as Isaiah said, a match that ignites newness. But it also is a sledgehammer, a ready tool to demolish the status quo too many, even the poor, accept as normal.

∼

"Comfort my people," God says, according to Isaiah 40, announcing return to the exiles, a return and resettlement after a generation or more in Babylonian exile. This is the comfort

---

[6] "The choice to live a life committed to the gospel message of liberation (salvation) is never based on some future reward in the hereafter. It is based on the meaning and purpose that praxis toward liberation gives to my life in the here-and-now." Miguel A. De La Torre, *Embracing Hopelessness* (Fortress Press, 2017), 52.

daughter Zion sought in the Book of Lamentations.[7] Now the comfort came as the exiles returned to repatriate their homeland and restart their future. As those beautiful feet crested the mountains toward the holy city, I expect even the weary exiles had a spring in their step. But then, when they saw Jerusalem, desolate and in ruin, the anticipation vanished. They wept. And they realized the hard work ahead of them to rebuild their beloved city.

In that same chapter the prophet offers a word on the sevenfold strength that their God would make available to them for the task at hand. This is the kind of strength that generates from a God who never tires; a supply of strength beyond what vigorous youth can offer or sustain. This strength looks like an eagle taking flight, an image of enduring energy.[8] Isaiah proclaims the eternal energy source available to the exiles as they return to ruins, as they must gather energy for the massive repair work—not only the labor involved in moving timber, stones, and metal to rebuild structures, but the work of imagining and constructing a new society.

This is the unending energy supply that fuels our hope. It is stirred in lament, then gathered up and deployed in the form of hope. The prophet says that hope will fund fresh imagination, and we will collaborate with the new thing God is doing across the landscape.[9] But the work of building a new city is long and hard. Implementing a new city plan will require the energy to hope and the energy for much hard work.

In the aftermath of return from exile in Babylon, many voices advocated for a plan for the new city. Among them,

---

[7] Scholars including Carol Newsome, Tod Linfelt, and Walter Brueggemann believe that 2 Isaiah is a response to Lamentations.

[8] The sevenfold strength is seen in the seven mentions of strength in Isaiah 40:28–31. The mention of something in the denomination of seven in the Hebrew language creates literary emphasis. In this pericope our attention is drawn to the sustainable energy on offer to those about to rebuild the ruined city.

[9] Isaiah 65 speaks to God doing a new thing, in particular 65:17ff.

Ezra and Nehemiah sponsored an exclusive society giving primacy to Jews with "pure seed," not intermingled by marriage to foreigners. Rebuilding the wall around Jerusalem topped their list of priorities. Their plan came from a sense of urgency. And a starting point for their strategic city plan was rooting out foreigners within and without.

Isaiah promoted an entirely different idea. He spoke of a wildly inclusive vision, a city that embraced eunuchs and foreigners as neighbors.[10] Not only were they to be welcomed by this reimagined city, he also wrote that foreigners should be included as full members of the city.

Prioritizing justice, even before the conversations about inclusion, mattered to Isaiah. In the third section of the prophetic book the focus is on the hard work of rebuilding the city. Here justice, which is always related to economic justice, is the cornerstone for the new city.[11] The prophet's instructions about justice seem to be embedded in ideas of equity, where all neighbors can access the benefits of the economy and make a good life within a well calibrated society. This is a strong start for exiles wanting to avoid the mistakes of the past. Construct an economically sound society, and it will be better for families and neighbors and less vulnerable in the geopolitical landscape.

The prophet continues the conversation about a strong economy, claiming jubilee as the standard practice in the new city. Jubilary actions, he adds, comfort those who previously mourned.[12] Those who cry out for comfort in Lamentations are given the balm of jubilee, of an economy that will allow them back in and provide them with a chance to survive. In

---

[10] According to a sermon Walter Brueggemann gave at Mars Hill Church in the summer of 2008, eunuchs represented those who capitulated to the empire and also had compromised sexuality. Advocating for their membership in the New City would have likely caused quite a stir, he said, talking about the passage.

[11] Isaiah 56:1.

[12] Isaiah 61:1–3.

this recalibrated economy good things and not bad will come their way.[13] That is the hope worthy of hard work.

Jubilee practitioners form a better economy—one that offers regular debt cancellation, fair and timely wages, and the capacity to keep land in the family for future generations—laying the foundation for a better society. In doing so, these practitioners offer healing to the bereft. They make it possible for everyone, from the exiles returning from Babylonian captivity to the mourning mothers left in the ruins of Jerusalem, to attain a fresh start in the renovated city. There is a kind of solidarity as they together survive in the city under construction. For those previously on the underside of things the enacted jubilee will create a stable economy and vistas of possibility.

That's when Isaiah notes a change in agency. While it is jubilee practitioners who will reset the economic landscape, it is *they*, the beneficiaries of these new policies, who will rebuild the ancient ruins, raise up what was devastated, and repair ruined cities.[14] If the policies enacted take root, then the women and men on the receiving end will not only experience transformation, a return to a full life, but become a transformational force in their own communities.

Jubilee policies are a movement from practitioners to neighbors as they transform into the agents of neighborhood investment projects. This is how Isaiah envisions an entire national transformation. One community at a time. Jubilee work is the catalyst for others to recover their life, energy, and agency, making communities viable and even vibrant.

∽

In our experience as practitioners, when people have real economic opportunity, including mechanisms of repair for the

---

[13] Walter Brueggemann describes this, Isaiah 61:3, as the move "from powerless indebtedness to the restoration of dignity and viability." (Walter Brueggemann, *Isaiah 40–66* (Westminster John Knox, 1998), 215.

[14] Isaiah 61:3b–4 "*They* will be called oaks of righteousness. . . . *They* shall build up. . . . *They* shall raise up, *They* shall repair the ruined cities."

hard years, they can surge back into public life. Our friends in Matara regained their sense of dignity as they planted and harvested their own fields. As they built homes. As they visited the local clinic to address malaria and a variety of ailments caused by malnourishment. They started small businesses. They took their produce to the local market. They bred and sold rabbits, herded goats and sold their meat, milked cows and sold to their neighbors. Amid all this activity, they entered public life.

Slowly they began to erode the prejudice of their neighbors with a community-works project. These Batwa families recognized that their land sat on prime real estate, right on the main road, making commerce easier for them. They noticed that their neighbors' plots sat far back from the road, making it nearly impossible for their neighbors to move goods back and forth. So the Batwa families proposed a new road be built along the edge of their land, facilitating greater accessibility for the neighbors. What this meant was gifting nearly 10 percent of their own land to a community project that would benefit the neighbors—a jubilary act indeed. What made this such a surprising initiative is that their neighbors hated the Batwa and took every opportunity to harass them. But the Batwa families sought and strategized for peace. So they proposed the road project, with one huge requirement. The Batwa, Hutu, and Tutsi neighbors would need to build it *together*.

The neighbors needed that new road. Necessity drove them to accept the offer of the Batwa. And so for the next six months, every Saturday morning, the men would gather and work together. At first the mornings were quiet, with the men not wanting interaction beyond preparing the way for the road. But months into the endeavor, the tenor changed. Claude joined them to find laughter and lots of conversation between them as they worked side by side. They had become friends.

So, not only did they build a new road, but they built a new way to be at peace with one another. A new kind of neighborliness formed as they put away former prejudices and embraced the new relationships emerging.

And during that first year of economic work and a public-work project, they also found themselves gradually accepted by the wider community. Three Batwa men were elected by their neighbors to the local council of judges. One mother was chosen as president of the Parent Teacher Association for the region. And the neighbors began to regularly visit the Batwa village, using the new road, to ask for advice on business matters because they noticed their successes.

All these years later, when we go to Matara for a Sunday celebration or other event, we see many neighbors sharing in festivities. There is a communal vitality—a more stable local market, better support for the nearby elementary and high schools, and less animosity and thieving between villages. Jubilee work was the hope-filled spark, but the Batwa women and men became agents of transformation for their own community. They were, to quote Isaiah, the "restorer of streets" where they lived.[15]

When the economy is humming along in a good direction, there is momentum. We learned in our development initiatives across the years that the economy was the foundation for all other enterprises. When we offered loans, training, and troubleshooting support for our Burundian partners, it cracked open wider work. A stronger economy or economic platform is a strong springboard for other public projects. Our porridge factory grew as we were intentional about the economic well-being of our farmers. The radio station, Kazoza FM, became a reliable tool for economic education and a sustainable venture as an outgrowth of our response to youth unemployment numbers. And the viability of the radio station allows us firm footing for other development opportunities.

The work of our bank has made it possible for many everyday business people to engage in their communities as

---

[15] Isaiah 58:12, echoed in 61:4.

leaders, offering small-scale repair in neighborhoods we could never reach.

An improved economy is a foundation on which other endeavors can build. Starting a fortified porridge factory created channels for distribution to vulnerable communities as well as a product for the market to offset costs. Our economic foundation generated ample credibility, allowing us to enter into conversations with the United Nations about leading a reforestation project. This created a partnership to benefit the climate in Burundi while benefiting over one hundred Batwa communities who live in the forest, restoring the dignity of the Batwa people who call this forest their original home. Economic work matters, even to community development organizations like ours.

Claude, being a very pro-business person, also encourages other fellow practitioners to look at where jobs can be created, where industries can be rehabilitated or expanded, or where more entry points into the economy can be made available for the more vulnerable members of a community. He shares his insight into constructing a wider economic landscape that is generative in as many directions as possible, for as many people as possible. Perhaps the prophets were not so concerned with the business side of the economy, but the structures of jubilee that they hold in common with people like Claude show a common commitment to make a viable life possible for communities by minding the economic dynamics and offering protective measures for those who, from time to time, are victims to the fluctuations of the economy.

From the prophetic voices I glean the imperative of tending to the most vulnerable, of not allowing the rich to eat them alive through their greed or apathy. While I contribute little to these conversations with practitioners about increased jobs or profits, I advocate for a holy attentiveness to those trying to survive on the margins, who need to be brought in from the cold of calcified and cruel economies.

What I have learned across the years is that jubilee both sets the trajectory for our economic imagination and offers tools for the formation of a social safety net. There is a clear-eyed awareness that economies do not stand still. They are precarious, fragile even, as external forces like foreign empires or nature impinge on their function, sometimes with violence. Internal realities like corruption, greed, and rising oligarchy add to the precarity.

It is jubilee that invites us to envision the most equitable economy possible, one that excludes no one. It is jubilee that invites us to repair economies that fall short. It is jubilee that rescues the vulnerable ones from the weight of indebtedness and resulting losses. And it is jubilee that calls us to in equal measure envision and emancipate.

In our work we've cycled through loss, lament, hope and hard work many times. And we cannot resist the siren song of the new city calling to us, imploring us to give jubilee another try—and another as we calibrate the economy as the groundwork necessary to construct a better society.

I recall the moment, sitting across the desk from Lydia, the nurse overseeing health outcomes for our primary school and feeding programs, while reviewing the month by month numbers of mothers, children, births. "No deaths in August, no deaths in July," she said as she scanned the pages with growing speed month by month. "None! No mothers or children died this year!"

I ran down the narrow hall, raced up the uneven stairs to Claude's office, interrupting his meeting. "No babies died this year!" I got out, amid a waterfall of tears. He shared my joyful shock at the news. It was possible to stanch infant and maternal mortality in our community! Even we were stunned when the kind of healthcare you imagine in the new city arrived in Bubanza. And each year our team works just as hard to expand that goodness to more mothers, more children, more families across the province. Jubilee is fueled by enduring—and contagious—energy!

9

The New City and the Work of Imagination

*I*n 2021, the United Nations put out a call for organizations interested in helping with a massive reforestation project in Burundi.[1] Kibira National Park, the previous hallowed hunting grounds of kings and home to the Batwa people, needed attention from the green practitioners. During years of civil war and the aftermath the forest—once thick with flora and fauna—fell prey to exploitation and degradation. The land displayed signs of climate change, its erosion detrimental to the overall environmental health of the small African nation.

Not only was the land endangered, the communities living in the forest, mostly Batwa, also struggled with fewer resources. Some faced displacement as well, like those families now in Matara.

Villages dotted the forest but most ringed its edges as communities tried to survive on small agriculture works that depleted the land and impeded the future growth necessary for a repaired landscape. Both the Burundian government and the United Nations knew this was not sustainable. So the quest began for an organization that could address reforestation, economic development for the more than one hundred communities, and inclusion of the Batwa people in the process.

---

[1] We began talks and application process in 2021 with the United Nations Community Development Fund. We were selected and signed the agreement with UNCDF in June 2022.

Given our work with Batwa families, we entered into the conversation with UN friends who'd observed Claude's on-the-ground work over the years. Of particular interest to them was our capacity for economic development based on the work we did in Matara and Bubanza, but also with Kazoza Bank. We had a track record. And we knew how to walk alongside people and cultivate economic capacity that lasted. But more important was our long and deep connection to the Batwa community. Years of joint effort allowed us to understand and collaborate with our Batwa friends, establishing trust as reliable partners. This, I believe, significantly factored in for the selection of our organization, Communities of Hope, to lead this reforestation project for the Kibira National Park.

Signing the contract with the UNCDF felt like a full circle moment in our development work. When nearly all we had to offer was our friendship, the Batwa welcomed us. Early on, we had little experience, but our good intentions and Claude's intuitive know-how built bridges.

At the beginning our friendship, over fifteen years ago, we invited Batwa leaders into our home for shared meals. Over plates piled high with stewed meat over rice and fried plantains we listened to their stories detailing their losses, when they were pushed off their traditional land, faced discrimination in employment and education, and endured the hardship of being undocumented in their own country. Over cases of soda they would tell us about weddings where they were consigned to tables on the edge of the celebration. After the meal the dishes they ate off of were cleared and tossed—no one wanted to use plates the Batwa had touched. After one of our shared meals, I recall one Batwa woman walking to our outdoor kitchen after the dishes were cleared from the table. When she saw all our dishes washed together she knew, she said, that we were really friends.

Over the next fifteen years we worked alongside the families, in both fields and the local markets, in both advocacy and ongoing conversation, to cultivate a viable life that was sustainable without us. We watched over one hundred babies born in Matara, our first community, and we were able to celebrate some of their birthdays together. We worked with our friends to make connections with the principal and teachers at the local primary school so that their children could attend school with better support, not repeating cycles of discrimination they had experienced in previous classrooms. We witnessed high-school graduations and watched some of these children go off to university, others becoming teachers and nurses in local villages. It is hard to imagine better outcomes for a community over time. But when we signed the contract with the United Nations, I realized a deeper dynamic circulating.

These families knew landlessness. Only their parents and grandparents remembered the forest's bounty. Now it lived only in Batwa dreams. The small communities that remained now live mostly on the far side of Kibira, forced outside the forest, where they now barely eke out a living. The memory of a land thick with promise receded season by season until it lingered only as a myth that inspired traditional songs. There was no longer any hope beyond survival.

Even for Burundians at large, Kibira National Park carries different connotations from the days of royal hunting grounds. Those legends collapse under the weight of decades of civil war crushing the forest. Now people speak of Kibira with a sad exhale, a place once glorious but now gone. It embodies loss, haunted by rebel ghosts and their remains. The depletion of Kibira is both physical and psychological. It is hope lost, an inaccessible Eden.

Deciding to partner with the United Nations on this massive restoration project, we plunged into deeper waters than ever before in our development work. Reforesting a national park and facilitating economic development for one hundred communities, all while centering the Batwa people and our conversations with them in the process—this was our stated mission. Achieving these aims would involve acute discernment as we navigated governmental agreements, international entities with vested interests in Kibira, as well as the intricacies of UN bureaucracy and politics. And yet, the inclusion of the Batwa in the project administration and in the benefits of Kibira's restoration hit me with jubilary force. It felt like ancient ripples of restoration reaching our contemporary shore.

We also knew the complexity and loss involved with the designation of a national forest. The conservation movement in the West pushed against Burundi in the early twentieth century; the impoverished nation was offered incentives to designate land, like Kibira Forest, as a national park. The agreement made with the International Union for Conservation of Nature followed the Yellowstone Model, which restricted human residence in the forest in the name of protection for the land, its flora, fauna, and wild life. This, combined with the civil war, forced most Batwa communities out of the forest—with no compensation.

The international community sought to preserve the land but destroyed the lives of those who lived in it. And the Burundian government was willing to sacrifice Batwa land for gains that benefited the ruling tribe. The Batwa lost no matter how the calculations were done. There remain some hold-outs, those that are clinging to the land because they have nowhere else to go, despite the increased pressure to leave and the deteriorating condition of the land due to climate change. Part of our remit with the UN has been to secure good land for these families outside the forest. Claude decided we would work hard to ensure the land was in the region and as close to the forest as legally permitted so that they didn't suffer further injury. But we know this is not perfect, and not even close to the justice the Batwa deserve.

This would not be a literal land return. There were no deeds to be handed over. Families would not be allowed to move into the forest to reclaim plots or start new gardens; the hold-outs could not stay. And no financial reparations would be directed to the tribe. But good land, as we could find it and afford it, would be purchased for as many families as possible.

And yet, the inclusion of Batwa leaders in the management of the national park marked official recognition of their sacred connection to this land. It was recognition that they were, in fact, the best forest keepers. Ensuring that they got a seat at the table where decisions about the future of the forest would be made returned some measure of control to the original inhabitants of land. And they would help determine which families got land. Their partnership in the land management of Kibira National Park incarnated aspects of jubilee: the return of stewardship to the Indigenous people, centering the Batwa people and their wisdom and labor on behalf of the land for the health of Burundi at large. It's not near enough. But maybe it is a mustard seed of jubilee for the Batwa, a small start now for a more full bloom of justice in generations to come.

Some of the best moments for a jubilee practitioner are when we advocate for and realize a handing over of the reins to the rightful stewards of the land, times when ceding control is holy. All our years of friendship with the Batwa families from Matara to Bubanza and beyond brought us to this position as facilitators of return. Our shared agreement would make us equal partners in the restorative work ahead. Jubilee would have its voice here and invite celebration. Justice would get a toehold.

～

One of the earliest lessons Claude and I learned regarding jubilee is that it isn't always or even often a strict reenactment of debt cancellation, emancipated slaves, or land returned to ancestral families. Unions organizing to protect workers' rights can be an embodiment of jubilee. A church, not a government, lessening or retiring medical debt is still experienced as jubilee by those in debt to the collection companies. There might be times when bankruptcy, with continued reforms, acts as a mechanism of jubilee, offering relief for those families saddled with insurmountable debt.

We understood from years of friendship with the Batwa communities that the losses were deep, that international organizations and their own government removed many of them from their land. That was empire at work. Lament was the prophetic response. We hope that their sitting at the decision-making table for the restoration of their ancestral home incarnates the beginning of jubilee.

Jesus understood he could not undo the Roman Empire, its violent economy, its land grabs, and worse. He was one man from Galilee. But he refused to do nothing. So he told his followers to begin breaking the cycle of indebtedness where they could—forgive debts owed to you right here in Bethany, in Bethlehem, in Nazareth, and even your unnamed village over the hill. Start! Begin embodying jubilee today, right where you stand on the outskirts of the Roman Empire. He knew the imperial economy needed to be dismantled. So he started where he was, like a stone tossed in the Sea of Galilee with the promise of ripples pushing ever outward. Being a jubilee practitioner feels like that a lot of the time, starting with the smallest inkling of equity or gesture of repair. But we start. We know it is not enough to have the Batwa leaders steward the forest or only to secure new plots of land for some families. We know. But we refuse to do nothing at all, to not step into jubilee somehow.

Many days it feels like I hold a single acorn in the palm of my hand. I close my eyes. I see a majestic oak tree with branches my grandchildren can swing from. I summon my prophetic hope and dare to imagine in a distant future a forest of oak trees. A new forest for a new city . . . and it will be inhabited by the Batwa once again. I don't know how this will be. They will bring their innovation, their labor, and their love to the jubilee-sized task. But all I can do from here is start. So we buy plots where we can, we give power to Batwa leaders where we can, and we start living congruent to the ways of jubilee now, even as it is too little today. There will be jubilee tomorrow. I believe it. I think Jesus did, too.

The New City and the Work of Imagination

Jubilee, for all its goodness, is not a panacea. For many years I thought it was, feeling discouraged, even defeated, when we fell short. Operating under the assumption that if rightly implemented, it would be the permanent solution for society set me up for added disappointment anytime our results were less than lasting, less than an ideal.

I began to recognize jubilee as a tool to break the fall of those teetering on catastrophic indebtedness or land loss. Jubilee, I knew, cast a vision for better economics while providing practices to calibrate current economic dynamics. But it wasn't until I learned jubilee was an evolving good rather than a stand-alone achievement to attain, that it was an economic program moving in concert with other societal building blocks (and often despite societal blockades), that I accepted its realistic limits—as well as its multivalent potentials. Jubilee economics is also neighbor support, washing all the dishes together, and conversations that lead to growing our common good.

Once I understood jubilee as movement among many toward the fullness of renewal, I began to relinquish wrong-sized expectations for better-sized application. This change has meant a willingness to see and savor moments when jubilee does succeed in freeing someone from deep debt, when jubilee calibrates the family income for a season, when jubilee creates a new opportunity at moving forward instead of succumbing to the perils of poverty. Each jubilary action—no matter how small—moves us toward the new city the prophet imagined.

∽

Within his book of lament and returns, walls and jubilee, Isaiah wrote an ode to a transformed landscape—a final description of Jerusalem as a new city worthy of delight. This city, once bent with corruption and injustice, is under construction. Economic justice is the newly established cornerstone, where jubilee practices shape and safeguard families in the ever-precarious economy.

As the path toward prosperity is set for all residents of the new city, other elements of the city begin working better. The land is awash in newness. The sound of weeping slowly subsides. In this new city, the prophet imagines, no one will die prematurely; babies survive childbirth and the early years; and the elderly live out the fullness of their days. Isaiah's hope-shaped testament envisions much-improved healthcare in this new city, and better conditions for workers, and food security to overcome malnourishment. These interconnected aspects are, in part, what forms a new city—a jubilee city worthy of our dreams.

Isaiah further imagines homes built and inhabited by families without the fear of foreclosure by predatory creditors. And the land they till, they harvest. They enjoy the fruits of their labor. No one is demanding their crop to feed foreign soldiers or hauling it away to satisfy an outstanding debt. His jubilary vision inspires our own. Maybe we can see better housing policy and availability of affordable homes, stronger agriculture programs and protections for farmers.

But this is just the beginning. Isaiah brims with hope for such newness that will, with the help of jubilee polices, transform Jerusalem and every city like it. But this work of imagination offers a call and invites a response. We are meant to join in the hopeful and hard work of building the new city. We are to reach for our hard hats and enter the construction site ready to do our part in the renovation. This is what it is to be a jubilee practitioner. We build the new city.

Jubilee is aspirational in the hands of Isaiah. His poetry sets the trajectory for our sacred imagination as practitioners. He points to the holy labor of jubilee economics, with real tools from antiquity for the hard work ahead for those who share in the dream of a new city. This is the work that frees families from the consequences of severe indebtedness, breaks cycles of debt in real time, shapes more equitable economies for better futures.

Even as I hold this vision, I live in a world of slow gains, empire grabs, lands lost, discrimination. It is both the lament and the vision that I hold. Isaiah's new city is not yet. But his vision remains, inspires, instructs, and provides a moral compass. He is my patron saint of community development work, articulating an agenda with both deep ancestral roots and high hopes for the work of crafting better tomorrows.

From the first, jubilee has been a catalyst in our work. At times we felt like early adopters of these ancient jubilary practices—those who believed that communities could be made new and purposeful once again with our successive efforts. We knew that jubilee required our creativity and commitment, and we gave it our best shot time and time again. In return, jubilee gifted us with tangible tools for our hands and poetic aspirations for our imaginations. We've been hooked, body and soul, to living our journey as jubilee practitioners.

We remind ourselves of the work *today.* Jesus announced his jubilee campaign begins now, today. And with that one word, we accepted the invitation. It was as though Jesus presented us with a template for consideration in community development, a place to start. The seed of *today,* of *jubilee,* burrowed deep in the loam of our life abroad, its roots intertwined with our highest hopes for Burundi.

Jesus, the prime example of a jubilee practitioner, pulled these practices from his Jewish ancestors. He made the economic program current by naming it as his platform. One Sabbath morning he announced that good news dawned on the neighbors assembled on the edge of the Sea of Galilee. Debts would start falling away. And he would go on to share, at a later date, a jubilee teaching in the context of a daily prayer: we begin today by forgiving the debts among ourselves. The good news begins with us practicing it, making it real in whatever measure is possible today.

We followed Jesus and the way of jubilee in our world, embodying it as best we could. If Isaiah helped us imagine jubilee, Jesus pushed us to practice it sooner rather than later. Jesus gave us the urgency of *today*. Forgive debts now leads us to set indebted prisoners free now, and then to save the mothers from falling into deeper poverty—and to create economic access for more families struggling to survive—*now*. Jesus, the revolutionary, certainly radicalized us along the way. Jesus believed jubilee could begin immediately. And we also believe that jubilee practice begins today.

∼

What we also know, today, is that jubilee is hard work, as all long-term transformational work is. Our world is awash with injustice, plutocrats, and corruption. As a result, we suffer incessant inequity, which includes heavy debt carried by most and too many in perpetual poverty. Add to this the lack of affordable housing, food insecurity, rising rates of infant and maternal mortality, increased suicide rates, and systemic racism and you see why people cry out for change *today*. Late-stage capitalism is not sustainable for society. I am not an economist with a better plan for a different socioeconomic structure. But I propose we begin preparing the ground for what is to come. That begins today with jubilee, which is like a spade turning the soil to ready us for a better future.

We have been lulled into believing that all that is available to us is the current economic structure, and that nothing different ahead is worthy of our hopes. Yet jubilee is the today that punctures our malaise, suggesting an end to our economic melancholy. It begins with imagining a new city, embracing the newness on tap with the requisite energy to try another way forward. Start small and forgive a debt owed to you. In doing so, you've set someone free—and embodied jubilee. You also subverted the empire, actively breaking the cycle of indebtedness. Imagine what you could do next!

The New City and the Work of Imagination

Can you envision a scenario in which you did not decide on a political candidate based on promised tax cuts? Instead, you calculate the cost of political agendas on your most vulnerable neighbors, on their safety and access to needed resources to survive an unforgiving economy. Then cast your vote accordingly, using your ballot as a tool to strengthen the entire neighborhood. Jubilee is a set of todays, a set of subversive moves curbing the excesses and cruelty of imperial economics while building a world more aligned with the new city.

Recently I shared a meal with a couple who had just purchased a modest home. The move left them with a townhouse to lease. Not needing anything more than enough to cover the monthly mortgage payment on the unit, a relatively small amount, they decided to set the rent accordingly. This meant that someone desperate for affordable housing would turn the key on a townhouse where their family would be safe and comfortable. Imagine charging less than market value for a rental property. Imagine the neighbors a bit frustrated because of what that does to the comps in their area. But these friends made good news possible for a family, even as it might have landed like hard news for other landlords. Here again we witness jubilee sensibilities critiquing systems as they stand, subverting the status quo in a hard housing landscape. Jubilee is not only community, state, or country. Jubilee is in our every *today*, and close to home.

I heard the story of a Mennonite woman in Canada who, upon learning she was living on lands stolen from Indigenous peoples in her territory, rewrote her will. In it she stated her intention to leave her house and parcel of land to the Indigenous tribal council in her region. This was her act of return, giving the deed back to the original stewards of the land. She trusted the elders would use the land for the benefit of the tribe, an act of righting old wrongs. Her imagination for the new city was influenced by jubilee, and she innovated accordingly.

Jubilee even made the evening news with word of former NFL football player turned farmer, Jason Brown. The highest paid center in the NFL, playing for the St. Louis Rams, Brown was offered $35 million for his next contract. He decided to walk away and purchase farmland in North Carolina. As he explains it, God called him to farm and feed people. Brown learned to farm for the sake of his community. To date, he has produced over 100,000 pounds of vegetables for his community.[2] He is fighting malnourishment and food insecurity, pushing back against food deserts with his bounty. That is the spirit of jubilee in action.

∼

Musician and frontman for U2, Bono, stepped into the spotlight as an activist for debt cancellation in 1999. He joined forces with academics, economists, and other advocates to promote the Jubilee 2000 Campaign, which aimed to relieve the heavy debt burden of highly indebted poor countries for 2000, the threshold of a new millennium.[3] The campaign idea was rooted in the jubilee canon, those ancient texts about large-scale debt forgiveness designed to deliver freedom for entire societies. Bono, already a friend of Africa, traveled the globe to countries that held debt notes, imploring leaders to consider canceling the debt so that these poor nations could begin the new millennium with true freedom to build a better future for their people. These indebted nations spend millions servicing debt to wealthy countries, and the hope was that relief would allow those monies instead to fund healthcare, education, clean-water initiatives, and the like.

---

[2] See more about Jason Brown's story at his website, https://wisdomforlife.org/firstfruitsfarm.

[3] The stated goal of the campaign was to reduce the $90 billion in debt owed by poor nations to $37 billion. This was not only for indebted African nations, but included those in the Middle East, South America, and Asia as well. But with Bono's high profile and clear connection to Africa, the popular understanding was that this was a campaign aimed at relief for Africans.

In his memoir, *Surrender*,[4] Bono writes about his work on the Jubilee 2000 Campaign. In his mind he was riffing on redemption songs, which was how he referred to the poetry of Isaiah and words of Jesus regarding jubilee practices. He leveraged his platform, connections, and friendships toward this initiative. He told President Clinton, "Economic slavery, it's a spiritual concept" and "'Redemption' I've discovered is an economic term."[5] He brought talk of jubilee right into the Oval Office.

In the years since news articles suggest a campaign with mixed reviews. Some claim it was a massive success, wiping out over $100 billion in debt owned by 35 of the poorest countries. Others say the goals were never fully met. In our conversation with others in African countries, we heard that the World Bank and IMF often inserted so many additional requirements for eligible countries to receive the debt relief, that it blunted the initial intent and effectiveness of the efforts of the jubilee activists. When it comes to actual debt forgiveness, the evidence is muddled. And then there is the added critique that Bono and his ilk embodied white saviorism and performative activism throughout the campaign, using justice work as a public-relations tool to sanitize their own reputations.

To learn how the Jubilee 2000 Campaign effected Burundi, Claude reached out to our contacts. Burundi, on the list of heavily indebted nations, was indeed in need of relief. He spoke with several people in the current and previous governments, those working in the ministry of finance, who would be privy to such negotiations. No one knew anything. He spoke with colleagues at the university, professors of economics, those who might have case studies on the efficacy of debt cancellation on the local economy or reports on the anticipated bounce back from such a massive fiscal release. Nothing. No one could find any evidence of debt cancellation.

---

[4] Bono, *Surrender: 40 Songs, One Story* (Knopf, 2022).
[5] Bono, 356.

What became clear to us was that no meaningful jubilee relief came to Burundi as a result of the global campaign. The silence of government ministers, the lack of studies and papers from the universities, told the sad story of no reprieve arriving to meet the need, despite the efforts of Bono and friends.

What did grow out of the Jubilee 2000 Campaign was a larger conversation about the morality of debt and those trapped in it due to geography, corrupt governments, and Western institutions that entangled entire nations in debt slavery. Some of us began investigating the complicity of our own national leaders in these exploitative dynamics for the first time. For all the flaws of this campaign, Bono did bring the ancient practice of jubilee into modern discussions of debt for another generation. He introduced jubilee language to a Christian cohort that did not know there was more to biblical economics than tithing and exhortations toward generosity.

Amid all that is fraught with the Jubilee 2000 Campaign effort, I still see Bono as an aspiring jubilee practitioner who believed beyond "concept" and lived into a call for jubilee *today*.

How might we try to practice jubilee economics with the imagination of Isaiah, the tools from our ancestors, and the work ethic of seasoned practitioners? I propose we begin with an understanding of jubilee tenets, their original context and purpose.

Among the tenets, Claude might well recommend you begin with love, an unabashed and clear-eyed love for the community you want to partner with in the long-term work of transformation. I recall how desperately he wanted me to fall in love with Burundi in the early days of our marriage. Looking back, I think he hoped that such a love would fuel our tandem labors as practitioners in his homeland. But as a young theologian, I entered through a different jubilee door than my husband.

Whichever threshold we cross, we are well served if we begin with a healthy dose of self-examination. The work of jubilee economics is both good and hard news, and it matters where you stand. Are you among the haves or the have-nots? Do you possess an accurate assessment of your own privilege due to your birthplace, skin color, the socioeconomic standing of your family, even your gender?

Are you more like Claude, who grew up in a poor family trying to survive a fragile economy of an underdeveloped country? Or did your family echo mine—a middle-class family with access to ample resources for a good life in one of the world's stronger economies? These, and many other intersecting factors, shape your social location. Once you know roughly where you are on the economic map, you can accept jubilee as potentially good news for your future, an opportunity to contribute to your community, a chance to relinquish for the sake of your neighbors, or choose to opt out of jubilee altogether.

My social location meant that jubilee challenged me. I had to accept the fact that I might be the one with a deed in my hand that needed to be given back to someone else. I needed to forgive a small debt owed to me in order for my neighbors to experience the liberation of jubilee economics. I needed to relinquish some things. I realized that just by virtue of my citizenship, I was complicit in my country's unjust economic system that locks people out of opportunity at home and locks them in poverty abroad. Therefore, the initial jubilee invitation for me included lament, confession, and change as I calibrated my understanding of what jubilee economics would require. These changes began to re-form me, enabling me to put emancipatory energy in the right direction.

Our Batwa friends in Matara began their jubilee arc as beneficiaries of pristine land for their families, freedom from economic enslavement, and small loans so they could begin anew. The thirty families were able to acclimate and settle in during that first year. Early into their second year of living into this new reality, Claude met with them for a training day. The assignment was to consider where they wanted to be in five years. He felt they were ready to do the critical work of dreaming and planning. He hung a white sheet between two trees and let them draw their dreams in ink. One sketched a cow. Others drew piles of vegetables representing robust harvests; another sketched marketplace stalls to sell homemade soap, fruit trees, and goats. One man drew a truck because, he said, he hoped to have enough milk from his cows to need a truck to haul it to the market.

These women and men believed that pathways to prosperity now existed for them. "This is what jubilee looks like," Claude said to them that day. "It is people having the capacity to plan for a better future, one that is possible for them with hard work and some support from their friends," he added. More than ten years later the Batwa community has achieved most of the dreams they drew that day. I wish someone had held onto that sheet as a testimony to their progress. But we know they have made their land and lives better thanks to jubilee efforts across the years together.

Looming large on the American landscape is what some call the Locust Generation.[6] These are Boomers, described as a cohort that eats through resources; they are living longer and therefore holding onto things longer.[7] Think jobs, leadership

---

[6] This term for the Boomer Generation is appearing on social media platforms like TikTok and Twitter (now called X). The term also has been used by Paul Begala in an article entitled "The Worst Generation," published in *Esquire*, and the likes of Thomas Friedman, who called the Boomers "hungry locusts" for eating through the abundance of their parents in "Two Generations: An American Story," *New York Times*, May 15, 2010.

[7] Boomers, living longer, need ample resources to fund their own lives. I am not advocating for them to give to the point of hampering their own well-being. But I think there are conversations to be had about holding too much for too long, or hoarding, which cripples the following generations.

positions, power. But also homes. Members of this generation keep their large family homes longer, even when children have grown and moved out. This has an impact on housing availability for younger, growing families. It also results in keeping housing prices high in some markets, making home ownership out of reach for many.

It occurs to me that there might be a jubilee invitation here for the many in this generation who have means and resources. There are opportunities to relinquish positions of power in churches, companies, and other institutions to create room for the next generation to lead. Boomers could consider their real-estate holdings and possibly downsize or divest large properties—to allow their children and grandchildren or other growing families or small intentional communities—to experience a jubilary boost, facilitating a move toward generational and communal viability. But opportunities for creative jubilary practices abound for all of us; we can bring blessing through acts of relinquishment in the spirit of jubilee. In a familiar text from the Hebrew Bible, the prophet Joel speaks of a God who will repay what the locust have eaten.[8] But what if human locusts themselves are transformed? What if repayment came sooner through acts of relinquishment? These are among a jubilee practitioner's dreams.

As for the generations that follow, what if we did not aspire to join the creditor class? What if we refused to work hard to fill up our own barns and hoard our resources, instead working hard to build the new city where we, alongside our neighbors, live viable lives? So much of scripture tells the story of struggle between debtors and creditors, the suffering at the hands of predatory economies and corrupt players. Why aspire to consolidate power and means when we might rather choose to be jubilee practitioners in a world in need of tangible good news.

It will come as no surprise that I return to the beloved prophet Isaiah's words for wisdom. He imagines a transformed

---

[8] Joel 2:25.

Israel beating its swords into plowshares, using metal for farming implements rather than violent pursuits. His wisdom asks us to imagine a tractor instead of a tank, a granary filled with wheat instead of an armory full of weapons, a tool to feed rather than a tool for fighting. And in that imaginative space I return, wondering how we can disarm debt.

Throughout human history debt has done violence to families and communities. Debt has waged war on the poorest among us, often robbing us of a good life or life at all. Can we turn our attention to dismantling the tactics that trap people in unending cycles of indebtedness? Can we consider jubilee close to home, calling a friend and forgiving a debt the friend owes us? Can we champion the legislative attempts at canceling student-loan debt, medical debt, and even the debt of the most impoverished nations?

Maybe one thing we disarm is our default assumption that failure to repay a debt is a moral failure of a person rather than a symptom of a broken system, one designed to serve the oligarchs and their interests. When we see jubilee as releasing people from debt, as reforming the system that entraps them, that's where the seeds of jubilee sensibilities start to sprout in us.

In his book on the history of debt, David Graeber closes with a word regarding jubilee. As late-stage capitalism gives way, he suggests jubilee might be the tool we've yet to try to address the economic duress of our times. It is worth a try, he says, but notes that it would be cataclysmic to our current economic order. And yet, he says, that is better than the utter collapse we can expect if we do not try at all.

Reading his analysis made me think of something I learned long ago from the discipline of ecology—*creative destruction*. A forest fire creates the conditions for new growth, for a reset that allows for health to return to the land. Could jubilee be that act of intentional creative cataclysm, destroying the status quo of current economies to open space for a new way forward? Like Graeber, I believe it is worth a try.

The New City and the Work of Imagination

Yes, it is hard to practice jubilee. And, yes, there isn't even one clear-cut model. Every instinct to move toward jubilary action invites our discernment, innovation, even courage. Every initiative requires long hours and long time-horizons to mete out such jubilary hope—not to mention a fair amount of humility for the trial-and-error nature of the enterprise. Yes, confrontation with complexities will stymie jubilee attempts; systems and detractors will try to thwart the work or make it less effective. Sometimes it can be hard to keep the hope of helping deliver the good news of jubilee at all.

We know, perhaps more than most, the rough terrain of jubilee. People doubt the idea of debt cancellation from the start, and current economic institutions make it nearly impossible to enact on any large scale. There is a reason—the vested interests of the economic elites, the billionaires and aspiring creditor class, who benefit from the economic structures as they are currently constructed. Structures that allow the rich to increase their wealth exponentially and with regularity. Structures that allow them to seize land from the poor at half the cost, that allow them to eke out labor from people struggling to survive the work they do for the rich.

But those kinds of economic edifices are built on an ethic that the prophets railed against. Even among the ancient kings were some who found reason to curb such economic behaviors that harmed the workers and the land, and failed to restore a battered people. Sadly, we in the modern era see these economic practices as normative and accept them as the only way interconnected economies can function. But that lack of imagination and perhaps even our capitulation to the empires of our day shine a light on the complicities shaping our economic logic that bars us from being better neighbors at a foundational level.

Yes, it is hard to practice jubilee. And yet, here we are, committed to jubilee.

Because what is the alternative? None of the good news for the poor that Jesus promised? No newness that Isaiah imagined for us? No deliverance from pharaonic economics and deeper neighborliness that Moses preached? No relief for the farmers and fishermen and women selling their goods at the local markets to feed their families? We just cannot accept a world without jubilee. For all its faults—all the hardships embedded in the practices, for all the uncertainty of the outcomes—we keep hope alive like an old wizened prophet unwilling to relinquish the dream of a new city where all are welcome, safe, and find the resources they need to live.

When our Batwa friends drew their dreams for the future of their families and their village, they drew outside the lines. What Claude noticed as he hoisted the white sheet between the trees is that they sketched out a desired future that included the neighboring villages. They imagined that in five years their neighbors would have access to more services, as the road they made together was complete. They drew large fields, dreaming that families down the road would experience bounty too. Our Batwa friends embodied jubilee. They could not imagine a good future ahead for them that did not also include the flourishing of their nearby neighbors.

The sheet, filling every last corner with sketched plans for future goodness, took Claude's breath away. It was a picture of how deeply the logic of the new city had taken root in them. Now we know why the Batwa leaders of Matara are known as the architects of hope.

It was as if our friends from Matara were rehearsing the wisdom of ancient civilizations, the wisdom of Moses before our eyes. Jubilee is a practice among neighbors for their mutual flourishing, because jubilee is a set of practices that, at its core, is deeply relational. Jubilee economics must be about neighbors, not numbers. And for all our time spent studying and practicing jubilee, it will always have an organic essence that we cannot exactly define or replicate, but that invited our surrender. Jubilee reminds us that debts can be forgiven, land can be restored, and tangible hope can grow again where it was once lost. We survive together when we calibrate the economy, and thus the city, for our shared future, in which all live a viable life.

Acknowledgments

This book offered Claude and me yet another opportunity for sustained reflection on our body of work over the past fifteen-plus years. Conversations happened in Burundi, the United States, and even Morocco. These conversations energized us, deepening our work and our love. Claude remains the man of my jubilary dreams, and I appreciate all our collaborations, including this one.

Is it appropriate to be effusive about your editor? When it comes to working with Lil Copan I cannot help but brim with words of gratitude, praise, and friendship. A masterful editor with a theological mind, a true partner from conception to completion, and a supportive presence through the rocky times. This book took a toll, but Lil was there to cheer, commiserate, and create a way forward when I could not see the next sentence. I needed every ounce of her intelligence and creativity for this project, and she delivered. I continue to be grateful for the good fortune of working with this amazing woman and friend.

I want to shout out my faithful literary agent, Rachelle Gardner. Years of collaboration have found us to be friends, and I appreciate the ways we've grown together across the many projects and seasons. She represents me, but she also knows me. I don't take our connection for granted; she continues to be the right partner, and it's a privilege to work together.

Special thanks to my stalwart friend and favorite conversation partner, D. L. Mayfield, who pushes me to think more deeply, highlights connections I nearly missed, and will not tolerate any lazy language on their watch. I don't think there is an idea I wrote about that we didn't workshop first. They make me a better human and a better writer. I could not imagine a day without our conversations about this feral world, our culinary exploits, and our delightful Corgis, Fern and Hutton

And thank you to Mark and Laura Shook and Community of Faith. Your support of Claude and me, our Batwa friends, and every venture in Burundi made so much jubilary goodness possible over our years of partnership. Thank you for trusting us through trial and error, and celebrating each good day with us. You allow us to have a solid foundation as we innovate and grow in our practice of jubilee in Burundi and beyond.